THE EPISTLES
— *of* —
JOHANNES G. WEISS
THE BIBLICAL VIEW

BY

JOHANNES G. WEISS

WestBow
PRESS
A DIVISION OF THOMAS NELSON

WestBow Press books may be ordered through booksellers or by contacting:

WestBow Press
A Division of Thomas Nelson
1663 Liberty Drive
Bloomington, IN 47403
www.westbowpress.com
1-(866) 928-1240

ISBN: 978-1-4497-6324-4 (sc)

Library of Congress Control Number: 2012915073

Printed in the United States of America

WestBow Press rev. date: 08/15/2012

TABLE OF CONTENTS

AUTHORITY

God's word is teaching us that Jesus is our example and that we should be like Him by doing what He says (Matthew 7:24, John 13:15). In Romans 5:5, Paul is talking about "like-mindedness according to Christ Jesus". This like-mindedness is actually a lifetime process and our sanctification which culminates at the end being changed like Him "in the twinkling of an eye".

On this concept I base my belief that when we teach the Word of God, we as teachers should always teach with authority, because this is what Jesus did. (Matthew 7:29). The teacher is a gift from God to the church (Ephesians 4:11) and their authority is based on the Word of God.

There is no wishy-washiness in the authority which our Lord requires from the teacher. They have to teach with authority. Words like "command" and "teach" are used (1 Timothy 4:11). Teach and exhort says 1 Timothy 6:2. However, do so in meekness "instructing" according to 2 Timothy 2:25. This meekness, however, does not mean that we cannot bring God's Word the way it is and what we know it means. It does not mean that we need to soften up the Word or tell the hearers that it is just our opinion. The way we teachers should instruct with meekness means that we realize all the time that we are teaching correctly by God's grace and not by our own wisdom!

I have personally heard some preachers and teachers stating that they do not claim to understand the subject completely or correctly. They want, apparently, to appear very humble! My reaction has been, "well you better not teach it then!" This kind of humility is false and caused by trying to be liked by their hearers. Apparently, this is how the scribes in Jesus' day were teaching. (Matthew 7:29).

We should teach God's Word with all the authority it requires and my experience is that some people will always object and call you a "know it all". Of course, there can be other traits in the teacher which will give this impression and the teacher should change and repent of this. A teacher should be of Godly character and lead a Godly life as a witness. If he does not live according to what he is teaching, do not listen to such a one. Of course, a Godly teacher is still human and subject to mistakes. However, I am convinced that when our Lord ordained a teacher to teach, He usually does not make false teachings. I believe if the teacher makes a mistake with some of his statements that the Lord can and will CLOSE THE EARS OF THE HEARERS, so that it will not do any damage. There is a biblical concept of "our words falling to the ground" (1 Samuel 3:19). This seems to happen many times.

When a Godly teacher discovers that he made a wrong statement, he should correct it. I discovered, for instance, that I made a wrong statement in some of my writings. Teaching about Hebrews 8:13, I said that the King James English word "decayed" meant rotten. But of course, The Law of God is good and cannot be rotten. The original meaning of the Greek word is: outdated, old. Therefore I repent and am sorry for this mistake.

2

I do invite any of you to let me know if you think that I departed from God's Word. I can and do want to learn from your comments. My own practical conclusion and advice on teaching is: if you are not sure about what God is saying and what it means, DO NOT TEACH ON IT!

GOD'S WAYS AND THOUGHTS

In Isaiah 55:8-9, God is telling us that His ways and thoughts are not like ours, but much higher. We humans seem to have a problem with that. Even Christians and followers of Jesus Christ are walking by our own ways and thoughts many times. Often we lack discernment about God's ways and thoughts, especially in difficult circumstances. A most important fact which does not seem to have an impact on many Christians is the fact, which God's Word teaches us, that He always wants to bring people to repentance and eternal life and that Jesus wants to use us to be a witness to this.

Jesus broke several rules and customs during His ministry. He warned us not to go by traditions of men. To mention some: working on the Sabbath and talking to a Samaritan woman. We can conclude that when Jesus broke the rules, it was for the purpose of evangelism and to bring people to repentance. The primary purpose of Jesus is and was to bring people to repentance. Since his ascension, he has given us the command to be a witness and a fruit producer. Even the Holy Spirit broke the rule not to interrupt the preacher and in Acts 10, He interrupted

Peter's sermon in order to fill the Gentiles with the power to be a witness.

Yes, God's ways and thoughts seem always to be guided by the idea to bring all people to repentance and eternal life. The important parable of the sower is repeated three times in the Gospels. It shows that God expects thirty, sixty or one hundred reproduction. If you are a Christian in a certain place, He wants many more Christians as a result of your witness. The amazing statement of Jesus in John 15:16 says "because by bearing much fruit, my Father is glorified" (John 15:8).

Jesus did spend His last moments here on earth to tell us of the Baptism with the Holy Spirit. This is in order to be an effective witness for Him everywhere (Acts 1:8). The situation today is like in the days of Noah, when every imagination of the thoughts of men was continuously evil (Genesis 6:5)! The Lord knows our imaginations and thoughts all the time and we walk in them often. Therefore, we need to be born again and righteous so that our righteousness will produce righteous thoughts (Job 12:5) and we can be much fruit producers.

AN URGENT WARNING

This warning is mainly directed to born again Christians, who are sincerely believing in our precious Savior Jesus Christ, but have not asked or experienced the promise of the Father (Acts 1:4-5).

Although many of you on my email list are already baptized with the Holy Spirit, I am asking you still to read this and use it as a message to your Christian acquaintances who are not baptized with the Holy Spirit, because we are so close to the end time, the time when Jesus will judge us all according to our works.

Jesus himself warned us all that there is a good possibility to run out of oil and not endure until the end (Matthew 25:1-12, the foolish virgins). If you are a born again believer, you do need the extra oil (power) according to the last words of Jesus in Acts 1:8. He called it "the Baptism with the Holy Spirit".

The widely taught doctrine that you receive this when you are saved, more or less automatically through sanctification, is very deceiving. The Bible does not teach or show this! Every time the Bible tells us about people receiving the Baptism with the Holy Spirit (Acts2, Acts 8, Acts 10 and Acts 19), it was to believers. Acts 19 happened some twenty six years after the Day of Pentecost. So there is no reason to assume that it stopped at any time.

According to Jesus words in John 14:17, we have the Holy Spirit WITH us as believers, but He will be IN us when we get baptized with the Holy Spirit. That it is possible to be a born again, water baptized believer for a period of time without being baptized with the Holy Spirit is sufficiently proven in Acts 8.

What we are seeing today is that there are many sincere believers continuously living in the state of the Samaritans in chapter 8. Without the baptism with the Holy Spirit, the Evil One is promoting this vigorously, because it makes you miss out on the power that Jesus promised in Acts 1:8. Therefore, all you Holy Spirit baptized friends should be also hammering on this subject and not be scared by the opposition. DEAR HOLY SPIRIT, BAPTIZED FRIEND, ARE YOU WILLING TO DO THIS?

The main scripture verse the opposition always quotes is in 1 Corinthians 12:13, "for by one Spirit we are all baptized into one body". However this verse is talking about a figurative baptism into the Body of Christ, which means the salvation experience, because the Holy Spirit is the one who brings you to salvation.

When Jesus spoke by His last words in Acts 1, He certainly was not talking about your salvation but about power which you need to be an effective witness! Please point this out to the opposition, so their eyes may be opened and the Body of Christ can become much stronger.

For those who yet need to be baptized with the Holy Spirit, you might ask "How"? It is very simple! Come to Jesus, very thirsty and drink by faith the Living Waters (John 7:37-39). Our Savior will not withhold it from you and you will receive it by faith, just like you received your salvation.

THE BAPTISM WITH THE HOLY SPIRIT

Acts 17:11 in the NIV Bible tells us how to be of a more noble character in God's sight. If that is a desire of our heart, we should examine the scriptures daily in order to determine what we hear is true and according to God's Word. I am inviting you all here to do this with me again on the most important subject of the Baptism with the Holy Spirit.

This occurrence which was going to happen was so important to Jesus that He spent His last words on earth to tell us about it (Acts 1:8). Naming this happening "the Baptism with the Holy Spirit" in Acts 1:4-5, He actually repeated the words of John the Baptist,, which we can find in three Gospels (Matthew 3:11, Mark 1:8, Luke 3:16). He already had told us in Luke 24:29 that He was going to send that which the Father had promised.

Does the baptism with the Holy Spirit pertain to the salvation of a person? Definitely not! Clearly Jesus said it would give the believing Apostles power to be witnesses for him in the whole world. The message was directed to the Apostles He had chosen already (Acts 1:3). They were already born again believers and even had received the Holy Spirit when Jesus had breathed on them (John

20:22). I believe that Jesus breathed on them to confirm the beginning of the New Covenant, which had started when He had shed His blood on Calvary (1 Corinthians 11:25). There needed to be a transition because they were saved under the old covenant.

We must understand that there are at least two dimensions of the Holy Spirit. Jesus speaking about the Holy Spirit said in John 14:17, "for He lives WITH you but shall in IN you". The parable of the ten virgins also indicate that there are two dimensions or volumes of the Holy Spirit, enough to make it until eternal life with Jesus on the end or not enough and insufficient to endure until the end. I understand from this that when you are born again through the work of the Holy Spirit, He comes to live WITH you. But when you are baptized with the Holy Spirit, He will be living IN you and empower you to be an effective witness.

To be an effective witness also entails that we will be able to live a more Godly life. The world must see that our witnessing is backed up by our own lives. They must see Christ in us! We must practice what we preach. This becomes possible through the Baptism with the Holy Spirit who will sanctify us. The Baptism with the Holy Spirit is truly a life changing experience! The 120 believers, who were obedient to Jesus' command to wait for it in Jerusalem, are the best proof of this. They reached the then know world with the gospel in an amazing short time. From a cowering bunch of people they turned into convincing witnesses almost at once!

I can testify to the same experience. Although I was born again when I was a fourteen-year-old during World War II in Holland, I was only a nominal bench warming Christian until 1970, when I and my whole family were baptized with the Holy Spirit. It changed our lives entirely and we became effective witnesses in the "utter most part of the world". The Holy Spirit gave us amazing power to evangelize and the Lord established many churches in the remote areas of the Philippines. They are bearing more fruit even today, as the Lord allowed me to observe during my last trip there in 2005. Praise God!

Jesus also referred to the baptism with the Holy Spirit as "the promise of the Father" probably indicating Joel 2:28. He had also mentioned the promise in Luke 24:49. We should ask ourselves and other Christians also, have you received the Holy Spirit? Some nineteen years after the day of Pentecost, Paul did ask that question in Ephesus to some disciples he had met there (Acts19:2). It is a very important question.

If your response is "no" or "I do not know", you must conclude that the Baptism with the Holy Spirit has not happened to you yet. If it has happened, you will know it because it changes your entire life! Are you a believer in Jesus Christ? Then He wants you to obey Him and wait for the promise of the Father. Acts 8 is definite proof that you can be a believer for a while and not have been baptized with the Holy Spirit. The Samaritans believed in Jesus and were water baptized but had to wait until Peter and John came from Jerusalem later on. The 120 followers of Jesus had to also wait for a while and so did the disciples in Ephesus.

The sad case is that today there are thousands and thousands of believers who never have been baptized with the Holy Spirit and either think that they are or do not feel a need for it. Some of them confuse the salvation experience with the Holy Spirit baptism. Others feel not worthy of it. What is required to receive it? Jesus said "Come unto me if you are thirsty". So you only need to believe and be thirsty enough to ask for it (John 7:37-39). That is a prayer request the Lord certainly will answer according to 1 John 5:14-15: "This is the confidence we have in approaching God; that if we ask anything according to His will, He hears us. And if we know that He hears us – whatever we ask, we know that we have what we ask of Him".

DEGENERATION

Instead of the word "degeneration", the Greek Bible uses the word "Apostasies". From this we get the word "Apostasy", which means falling away. What is meant by falling away? The Bible means falling away from sound doctrine and biblical practices. This word "apostasies" is mentioned in 2 Thessalonians 2:3. This verse predicts the great falling away before the second coming of our Lord Jesus, which is referred to in 2 Thessalonians 1:10. I am convinced that today we are experiencing this "apostasy" in increasing measure. That is why I feel compelled to write this article.

I believe what is doing the greatest damage to the Christian churches is the practice of clericalism. If you do not know what this word means, the old Webster dictionary gives the following accurate definition of that word: "an effort and system of ordained clergy, to maintain influence and power". Today the concept of the priesthood of all believers has practically flown out of the window.

At the beginning of the reformation, in the 1500's, the concept of the priesthood of all believers was very strong. But today, although many give lip service to this concept, the application of this idea is greatly absent. Today, we have mainly pastors in churches, which are doing and controlling everything.

To begin with, the word "clergy" is not found in the Bible, but the word "laos" (laity) describes the body of New Testament believers. There are deacons, elders, bishops and the word pastor is also mentioned. However, that title is mentioned only one time in Ephesians 4:11, as opposed to the word of multiple "elders". Our Lord tells us that He has provided the church with apostles, prophets, evangelists, teachers and pastors (Ephesians 4:11). But our Lord also mentions the five-fold ministry in 1 Corinthians 12:28.

The word Bishop is mentioned in 1 Timothy 3:1-2 and in Titus 1:7. In both cases, it is just another word for elder or overseer. We also need to take heed of the required qualifications, listed there for this job. Today, most churches have pastors and the larger ones have also assistant pastors. They are under the authority of the "head pastors". In the New Testament Church there was no other head than Jesus Christ Himself.

Many churches do have a board of elders but they are usually chosen by a so-called democratic voting process. Most of the time the major consideration as eligibility for the job is whether you are a faithful tither who is inclined to obey the Pastor. The biblical requirements and the ordination from the Lord are usually ignored. Most pastors who will read this will probably strongly deny that this is speaking about their church. But which pastor is actually looking for a God ordained five-fold ministry today? Not many! This has and still is having a devastating effect on the universal Church. We are mainly producing bench-warmers out of the congregation and people who want to be entertained. There are now millions of Christians who never have won one single soul to Christ. They are like branches that are separated from the vine and will be gathered to be burned (John 15:6) because they are not bearing fruit. The meaning of fruit-bearing is to produce seed for propagation and multiplication.

What a serious warning is this for us that you my reader may take heed, if it applies to you!

P.S. The major qualification to become a pastor today seems to be a college education followed by seminary. Is this the only way to produce spirituality in a person? The evidence strongly points that this is not the case!

DESIRABLE RICHES

As sinful human beings, we seem always to be striving to gain more finances and possessions. We are aiming to be more comfortable or to have more power. We are even taught that unless you have this ambition, you are a failure. There is a very popular saying among Wesleyan Christians and others: "Make all you can, save all you can and give all you can". It sounds so good and Godly, but is it really?

For the first part, Jesus' words of Matthew 19:24 come to my mind. "It is easier for a camel to go through the eye of a needle than for a rich man to enter the Kingdom of God". Do we really heed this very serious warning? The Lord considers this subject of "gaining" so important that He repeats it twice in His saying of Matthew 16:26 and Mark 8:36. "For what shall it profit a man if he gains the whole world and loses his soul"? Do we as followers of Christ have much regard for our souls?

As far as saving all you can is concerned, the story of the rich fool should be a serious lesson for us (Luke 12:16). Then, the Lord's teaching from Matthew 6:19-20, "lay not up for yourselves treasures upon earth" is very plain. That is not to say that you should never save. Joseph was led by the Lord to lay up for the seven years of famine. But we should only do it as led by the Holy Spirit.

To give all you can is not the right idea either, although it sounds very spiritual. There is strife in this idea and in following this concept you feel compulsion! We never should give out of compulsion (2 Corinthians 9:7). As opposed to compulsion, we should give with a cheerful heart. It will become naturally for us to give our whole self cheerfully when we become Godly in obeying God's Word (Romans 12:1).

Can volunteer austerity be Godly? It can be, but not necessarily so! It depends on our motives. I used to be a real Dutch cheapskate. However, my motive was not to please the Lord but to gain more for myself. I pray that the Lord will eliminate this selfishness in me. In ancient times, there rose up a sect called the Ascetics, followers of an old hermit who lived on roots and berries, thinking that this would make him super spiritual. They preached and enforced complete self denial. In their rigid self denial, they actually did do serious damage to their bodies and were in fact very ungodly! However, volunteer austerity, led by the Holy Spirit can be a great help to conquer our selfishness. Our motive then should be that we can do more for others with our God-given resources.

To be rich towards God should be our goal instead of gathering riches for ourselves. Contentment with what the Lord has provided for us is also much needed. 1 Timothy 6:6-8 says "Godliness with contentment is great gain and to be content with food and raiment. If we seek first the Kingdom of God, all things will be added unto us and we will prosper even as our souls prosper. When the Lord pours out His blessings of abundance upon us, riches will not become a curse and a cause of losing our soul. A final thought: The Lord usually will bless us only to the extent of which we can deal with. This is in order not to tempt us beyond our endurance. Praise His Holy Name!

DISCERNMENT

What we commonly call discernment, the Bible calls it distinguishing between Spirits (1 Corinthians 12:10). This makes me wonder, when we do show discernment, spirits are involved in most of those cases. In general, Christians seem to have so little insight into the Spirit world. The Bible lifts the tip of the veil covering the Spirit world only a few times. It seems that our Heavenly Father does not want us to have a complete knowledge of what is going on in the Spirit world. We might not be able to cope with a complete knowledge and understanding of the Spirit world.

There seems to be Christians nowadays who are very occupied with "spiritual warfare". Most of them mainly seem to base their ideas on Daniel 10:13 and 20, which is revealing the Prince of Persia. Of course, the New Testament does tell us about spiritual warfare. "For we wrestle not against flesh and blood, but against principalities, against power, against rulers of the darkness of this world, against spiritual wickedness in high places" (Ephesians 6:12). However, I find most of the spiritual warfare teachings more carnal than spiritual. Some of the writers seem to forget that our God provided us with armor and weapons, so that our victory is assured. In Christ we are safe!

Overall, there seem to be a great lack of spiritual discernment among Christians today. This is very harmful to the individual and the church. Jesus warned us several times and especially in the last day, deception will be rampant. "Many false prophets shall arise and shall deceive many." (Matthew 24:11).

Spiritual discernment has to do most of all with the hearing of God's Word with our spiritual ears. I am convinced that even in the most mundane and ordinary things of life, the Holy Spirit wants to guide us. But we do not hear His whispering small voice most of the time. I must confess that only sometimes do I hear God's voice, but not often enough. This is caused by our fleshly carnality and the idea that we ourselves can figure out what is best for us. Our spiritual ears seem to be closed most of the time.

In the matter of guidance, it is our own fault that we do not hear Him. Warnings from the Holy Spirit are most ignored and sometimes with devastating consequences. In my own life, looking back, I discerned several occasions when that happened to me. However, through God's great mercy, I survived the disasters and learned from it.

Christians are still prone to deception and especially self-deception. There are three spiritual forces in the universe: God's, Satan's and the Human Spirit. Our own human spirit deceives us often. Just look at 1 John 1:8, "If we say we have no sin, we deceive ourselves and the truth is not in us. The first two chapters of 1 John have six references to self deception: John 1:6, 8, 10 and John 2: 4, 6, 9. There are many warnings against self-deception. I find the scripture most direct is Galatians 6:3, "For if a man thinks himself to be something, when he is nothing, he deceives himself". Therefore self-deception seems to be caused mainly by pride. Finally James 1:22 is telling us that if we are hearers of the Word only and not doers, we deceive ourselves.

There are remarkable stories in the Bible about Godly men who were still deceived and did not discern God's warnings. 2 Chronicles 18 shows godly King Jehoshaphat still making wrong decisions to ally with King Asap, but still insisting for Asap to inquire from God first! Then there is 1Chronicles 21:1 where Satan provoked David to number Israel and the Lord was very angry!

The purpose of this exhortation is that you can and will avoid disasters caused by non-discernment like the disasters I experienced in my life. You can do this by tuning your spiritual ears to discern the voice of the Holy Spirit. How do we do that? By loving and obeying God more and more, having the fear of God in us and practicing daily godly habits like Bible reading and meditation with praying. May the Lord bless you all by perceiving the gift of distinguishing of Spirits in your daily lives.

DIVINE GUIDANCE

God's Word, the Bible, tells us a lot about the Lord's guidance. There are cases listed we could consider as unconditional guidance. However, most promises of the Lord on guidance are conditional. Isaiah 58:11 is one of the clearest examples of this: "And the Lord shall guide thee continually. And satisfy thy soul in drought. And make fat thy bones: and thou shalt be like a watered garden. And like a spring of water, whose waters fail not". But then in verse 9, it states a big "IF" and in the context of all the verses, it shows that His guidance depends a whole lot on our righteous conduct.

I quoted the part of making fat my bones to another believer one day, more or less as an excuse for my overweight. His response was correct and quick however. "But the Lord is not talking about all the blubber under your skin"! Psalm 37:3 says: "The steps of a GOOD MAN are ordered by the Lord". The whole Word of God makes clear that in order to receive divine guidance; one has to have an obedient and sincere heart with a desire to be guided by the Lord. Proverbs 11:3 states "The integrity of the upright shall guide them; but the perverseness of transgressors of transgressors shall destroy them".

Bob Mumford's teaching during the charismatic renewal in 1970 has helped me a lot. Proverbs 11:8 says that the righteous are delivered out of trouble and the wicked will take their place. Note that the Lord is not saying that we will not get into trouble, but He will deliver us out of trouble. Trial and error is one of the principles of divine guidance which was clearly shown in Luke's writings about Paul's missionary travel (Acts 16-9). It seems that because of our imperfection, the Holy Spirit has to restrain us sometimes!

The books of Psalms contain many verses on God's guidance. Here I will list some of them: Psalm 23:2, 25:5-9, 31:3, 32:8, 48:14, 61:2, 73:24, 78:52, 107:7 and Psalm 139:9-10, 24. During my life, many people have told me that they never have heard from the Lord or experienced His guidance. Some were even critical when they heard someone else state "the Lord told me". However, it is a biblical and proven fact that the Lord sometimes speaks to His children either with an audible or subjective still voice. When your relationship with the Lord is good, you can and will hear His voice sometimes to guide you. Isaiah 30:21 says "and thine ears shall hear a word behind thee, saying this is the way, walk ye in it, when you turn to the right hand and when you turn to the left".

Yes, sometimes the Lord speaks to His children even with an audible voice! He did that to Paul and I have heard some godly people testify that it happened to them. To me, it was always the still small inner voice, an internal subjective and distinct voice in my Spirit just as clear as if it had been audible. The last time when I experienced His voice was in 2001, when I was almost dying in the hospital. After a long severe struggle, I was finally submitting myself to die. Then I heard the Lord speak clearly in King James

English, "I have not called you up yonder yet!" From that time I began to recover.

Bob Mumford had a very clear way to explain how we should be guided in our decisions. There are three beacon lights and all three should be lined up. The first one: is the guidance in line with God's word? Secondly: does it witness with the Holy Spirit's witness inside of you? Thirdly, does it fall into place with the practical circumstances? If the three do not line up, do not assume that your guidance came from the Lord. The last beacon light, the circumstances, can be very tricky however. Sometimes the wind can be contrary, but the Lord is testing you and wants you by faith to overcome the difficulty. While other times it is the restraint from the Lord. You, yourself, have to find out what it is.

Some severe hindrances to receive divine guidance are: disobedience, mistrust, selfishness and stubbornness. Ask the Lord for help and forgiveness. Did you know that the Lord is asking you in Jeremiah 3:4 "Wilt thou not from this time cry unto me, My Father, thou are the guide of my Youth?

BIBLICAL FAITH

I am using the word "biblical" because there seems to be a lot of teachings on faith which are not biblical and wrong. The Rhema bible school in the USA, under guidance of Kenneth Hagin and Kenneth Copeland, especially seem to be prone to wrong teachings on faith. They are making a separate entity of faith as a mysterious force which God Himself also had to use to create the universe! This is in conflict with the Bible which states that Jesus Himself is "the author and finisher of our faith (Hebrews 12:2)". By assuming that God Himself has to use faith to do His work, they are pulling God down to our human level and elevating men to God's level! For sure, nowhere in the Bible when the word faith is used, is there any indication that our God needs faith for Himself. He is the creator (author) of faith, all powerful and total sovereign.

I heard Kenneth Copeland even tell people on TV that God's Word was mistakenly translated when Jesus said in Mark 11:22 "have faith in God". He claimed that it should say "have the faith of God or the God-kind of faith". They even printed a Bible incorporating this change and started a whole doctrine on how we also can and should use this mysterious force!

Most of the reputable translations of the Bible are using the word "in" for the Greek word "en". It is true that sometimes it could be translated as "of". However according to most Greek scholars, if there is a subject involved, it has to be translated as "in". What probably happened here is that Copeland had a preconceived idea about faith and to fit his thinking he changed the normal translation!

Having settled this, let us look at the biblical definition of faith. Hebrews 11:1 states: "Faith is the substance of things hoped for, the evidence of things not seen". Remarkably, this seems to mix faith with hope. Indeed, when we study the word hope in the New Testament especially, we can detect that it means "being sure of something", rather than having doubt. While the worldly meaning of the word "hope" indicates that "maybe or maybe not", for instance "our blessed hope" of Titus 2:13 indicates that we surely believe that Jesus is coming back for us. In Hebrews 10:23, the Greek version shows the word "elpo" (hope) instead of faith. The King James translates it as faith however. Therefore, it is important that we see the word hope as being a sure thing, the same as faith. "Christ in you the hope of glory" (Colossians 1:27).

So the whole definition of faith in Hebrew 11:1 speaks of surety (substance, evidence and hope). In the world, the word "faith" is also used in place of religion. People ask "of what kind of faith are you?" I do not mean to cover this aspect of faith in this article, but let us continue what biblical faith is.

Since Jesus is the author and finisher of our faith, we should know how we can obtain it. Well, the main method our God is using for dispensing faith is stated in Romans 10:17, "Faith cometh by hearing and hearing by the Word of God". Of course, we have now God's Word in the printed Bible. Therefore, we can assume that I also mean reading

God's Word. God also has promised that in the latter days He will write His laws in our mind and hearts (Hebrews 9:16).

A remarkable scripture is that God says that He gives everyone a measure of faith (Romans 12:3). That might be the start of a human walking with God. It seems clear that then God expects us to use this measure of faith so that it will get stronger. Remember also that God tells us that it is impossible to please Him without faith (Hebrews 11:6). Faith is absolutely required for everything in a Christian's life!

At first, a man becomes saved through faith: "by faith you are saved through faith (Ephesians 2:8). Then we will obtain "righteousness"; "The righteousness which is of God by faith (Philippians 3:9)". However, we are required by God to "live by faith". He wrote that several times in the Old Testament as well in the New Testament. "The just shall live by faith" (Habakkuk 3:4; Hebrews 10:38).

Living by faith has to show evidence by having "works and deeds". James 2:26 states: "Faith without works is dead" and "such dead faith cannot save you!" (James 2:14). God is teaching us "Oh vain men!" (James 2:20) that if there is no evidence of "works", you can assume that here is something vitally missing and wrong with your faith.

Finally, something very interesting about faith I have to point out. Our Father God lists "faith" both as a fruit of the Holy Spirit (Galatians 5:22) and as a gift of the Spirit in 1 Corinthians 12:9. Now fruit will take some time to grow into maturity. While the Lord is helping you with growing this fruit, we should promote it to grow stronger by exercising it. We do that by showing trust in God. The gift of faith is probably given by God on occasion, instantaneously to accomplish something especially outstanding like a supernatural miracle. God decides to whom and when He gives this special gift. At least this is my understanding.

I am closing this meditation on biblical faith with the exhortation of Hebrews 10:23. "Let us hold fast the profession of our faith (hope) without wavering; for He is faithful that promised".

FAITH

God's Word tells us that "the just shall live by faith" (Romans 1:17 and Habakkuk 2:4). But we must know who are the just. According to Romans 10:9-10, we are justified when we believe with our heart that Jesus is Lord and confess it with our mouth. Do you qualify under this condition? Then the next question is "What is faith"? Also on this, the Lord gives us a clear definition. "Now faith is the substance of things hoped for, the evidence of things not seen" (Hebrews 11:1). The NIV translation looks like this: Faith is being sure of things hoped for and certain of what we do not see".

The next thing that we as believers need to know is: how do we obtain this faith? Well, our Lord tells the brethren that He has given each one the measure of faith (Romans 12:3). In addition, Romans 10:17 says, "faith cometh by hearing and hearing the Word of God". Therefore, we should realize that we cannot work up faith by ourselves. It has to come from God.

Faith is an absolute necessity for a Christian. Hebrews 11:6 tells us that without faith it is impossible to please God. Do you want to please God? I sure hope so! We have to use our measure of faith knowing that God has given it to us. If you feel weak in your faith, you can ask the

Lord to increase it. The Father of the demoniac son and the Apostles did ask for an increased faith and the Lord honored it.

Also, we should exercise our measure of faith so that it can grow and get stronger. It will atrophy if we do not exercise it. When the Apostles asked Jesus how to do the works of God, Jesus' answer was: "This is the work of God that you believe in Him who He has sent" (John 6:28). It is our fundamental duty to exercise our faith daily. We cannot receive anything from the Lord without faith (James 1:6-7).

Jesus told us to have faith in God. All major Bible translations say faith "in" God because the Greek grammar requires the Greek word "pivstin" to be translated as "in" when it points to a subject. Otherwise, it can be translated as "of", according to Greek language scholars. However, some well known radio and television evangelists seem to have different Bibles and teach that we should have the faith "of" God. Then they base a whole false doctrine on this mysterious force called faith, which even God had to have in order to create everything. They ignore the fact that God is all powerful, sovereign and is the giver of faith. He does not need faith Himself! But they insist that when we do have this mysterious faith "of" God, we can do much of what God can do. The result of this teaching is that our God is brought down to a human level and man's capacity is glorified. It diminishes the idea that God is all powerful and completely sovereign. He is the "giver of faith" and does not need faith Himself!

Scripture lists faith in Galatians 5:22 as part of the seven Fruits of the Spirit, but also as one of the nine gifts of the Spirit in 1 Corinthians 12:9. I gather from this, that as a fruit, it starts small and must grow in maturity over time. There is no instant fruit! With a gift of faith, there may be spurts of extra faith into a believer to be used to accomplish miracles in others.

In conclusion, we must remember to make sure to be "found in Him", not having a righteousness of our own, which is of the law, but that which is through faith of Christ, the righteousness which is of God by faith. Philippians 3:9. Therefore being justified by faith, we have peace with God through our Lord Jesus Christ. My prayer is that we may have this peace in abundance.

FEAR NOT

And the angel (Gabriel) said to Mary, "Fear not Mary, for thou has found favor with God" (Luke 1:30). At this Christmas season, God's Word is admonishing all Christians several times "fear not" because we as followers of Jesus have also found favor in God's sight. Hallelujah! Most of us have a foreboding feeling caused by the dark, bad times the world is in. But our Lord is saying "Fear not!"

This encouraging message is found many times in God's Word, starting with Abraham in Genesis 15:1. We can find it in Isaiah 43:1-5, Zeph. 3:15, Matt. 14:27, 17:7, Luke 1:13, 30 and ending with the angels message to the shepherds in the filed. "Fear not, for behold I bring you good tidings of great joy, which shall be to all people. For unto you is born this day, in the city of David, a Savior, which is Christ the Lord!"

In January 2004, I wrote an article on the subject of fear. However lately, the Holy Spirit has been conveying a lot more to me about this human emotion. We need to understand that our Lord has created us with a capacity to fear. He equipped our bodies with adrenalin, which can function as a life-saving warning system for life-threatening dangers. But as with so many good things which God has created, Satan uses it for our hurt sometimes by perverting our fear. Normal human fear can turn into unhealthy phobias, for instance.

Our Lord, therefore, is not directing his admonition not to fear to us against our normal life-saving capacity to discern danger. He is saying His "fear not" to let us know that He is in the events occurring and we have to trust that it will work out for our good.

The biblical concept of the fear of God, however, is a different matter and an absolute necessity for a Christian. It accomplishes many needed and good things in our lives. I will list here twelve major ones:

1. First of all, it will fill us with awe and wonder about the amazing Heavenly Father we have! (Job 37:22-24)
2. It preserves our lives as we obey Him. (Deut. 6:24, Prov. 10.27, 14:27)
3. It creates a hedge and many blessings for us. (Job 1:9-10)
4. God's eye will be on us and keep our souls from death and alive in famine. (Ps. 33:18-19)
5. It is the beginning of wisdom. (Prov. 9:10, Ps. 111:10)
6. It is the beginning of knowledge. (Prov. 1:7)
7. It instructs us in wisdom. (Prov. 15:33)
8. It fulfills the desire of all who fear Him (Ps. 145:19)
9. It causes abundant goodness (Ps. 31:19, 34:9)
10. The sun of righteousness will rise with healing in His wings. (Mal. 4:3)
11. Salvation—Eternal life for those who fear Him. (Ps. 85:9)
12. Restrains you from doing evil. (Prov. 16:6)

Number 12 especially, has kept me personally from committing serious sins. Proverbs 16:6 says "By the fear of the Lord men depart from evil.

I need again to point out that there is a wrong application of human fear, which can prevent us from doing God's will. It can be debilitating, demoralizing and destroy you. That is why the Lord is assuring us in 2 Timothy 1:7 "For God has not given you a spirit of fear; but of power and of love and of a sound mind". Then in I John 4:19 the Lord states "There is no fear in love, but perfect love casteth out fear: because fear hath torment. He that feareth is not made perfect in love".

Do you have a problem with fear? Do you want to learn the fear of God? Deuteronomy 4:10 gives us the solution: "Gather me the people together and I will make them hear my Words, that they may learn to fear me all the days upon the earth and that they may teach their children".

So when you gather together this Christmas season, study God's Word and be much blessed. Merry Christmas!

THE FEAR OF GOD

The common meaning of the word "fear" is being afraid of something. But right from the start, we must understand that we as God's children should have a trusting and loving relationship with our Heavenly Father and have no fear for him. There are therefore two kinds of fear: the ordinary, fleshly kind, which our Creator has built into us for our self-preservation and the biblical fear of God. The first kind works mainly through our adrenaline system and can be either good or bad, depending on what we are afraid for and how we react to it. The Godly fear is commanded by many scriptures of God in His Word. I will quote here just a few: Deut.10:12 "And now Israel, what does the Lord they God require of thee, but to fear the Lord thy God, to walk in all His ways and to love Him and to serve Him with all thy heart and with all thy soul".

This connects fear with the Lord's first commandment. Psalm 33:8 says "Let all the earth fear the Lord; let all the inhabitants of the world stand in awe of Him". Here we see that godly fear also means to be in awe and have reverence for the Lord. The New Testament also tells us in several places to have the fear of God. Ephesians 4:1 "Let us therefore fear, lest a promise being left us of entering into

His rest, any of you seem to come short of it". The context of this verse we find in the end of chapter 3. It shows that this fear is the fear for loosing our salvation. Another difference between the human kind of fear and the Godly kind is that we have to learn to obtain the fear of God and we have to learn it through hearing God's Words. The remarkable verse of Deuteronomy 4:10 tell us that. "Gather me the people together and I will make them hear My Words that they may learn to fear me all the days that they shall live upon the earth and that they may teach their children". The fear of God has several promised benefits connected to it: it prolongs our days (Proverbs 10:27); we will have endurance (Isaiah 12:14); it is connected to divine guidance and peace (Psalm 25:12); it is a condition for acceptance by God (Acts 10:35); God's mercy is connected to it (Luke 1:50) and it gives you light in the darkness (Isaiah 50:10). It is also both the beginning of wisdom (Psalm 111:10) and wisdom itself (Job 28:28). The way I see how the fear of God works in providing all those benefits is that it keeps you from yielding too many temptations and foolish, ungodly decisions. The fear for the consequences of your willful sin can keep you out of a lot of trouble. I must also say that this knowledge came through my personal experiences. Many times the Lord has provided a way to escape the temptation through the fear for the consequences, confirming 1 Cor. 10:13.

A verse that at first look seems to be a contradiction to the Lord's will, to have the fear of God, is 1 John 4:18. "There is no fear in love; but perfect love casteth out fear: because fear has torment. He that feareth is not made perfect in love". However, as I came to understand this verse, God is saying, if you were perfect in love, fear would not be needed. The Holy Spirit did ask me "Which one of you is perfect in Love?" I had to admit that Jesus is the only one who was and is perfect in love.

Another verse in the New Testament which speaks against fear is 2 Timothy 1:7. "For God has not given us the spirit of fear but of power and of love and of a sound mind". From this context, we can conclude that the Lord is speaking here of not being afraid or timid concerning our gifts and the gospel. He was warning Timothy not to be ashamed in verse 8.

The fear of God is closely connected to the love of God, because He chastises us as His sons in His great love. Therefore, we need to have both the love of God and the fear of God manifested in our lives.

FATHER KNOWS BEST

This concept is entirely based on trust and trust is the ultimate form of honoring someone. It is a necessary ingredient in the love relationship between father and child. God's Word speaks a lot about this trust and requires it in our relationship with Him because He is our Heavenly Father. The main reason why Jesus used little children as an example in Matthew 18:3 is the fact that a little child has a complete trust in his parents and totally relies on them. He said "Unless you be converted and become as little children, you shall not enter the Kingdom of Heaven". A normal child does not have fear or worry about his/her needs, but assumes naturally that all needs will be supplied.

The trouble with us so called "grown-ups" is that we think most of the time we are capable to figure out what we need and what we can do to bring it about. I have come to the conclusion and am convicted that most of us acknowledge "father knows best" with our mind and lips, but in our hearts and our spirit, we do not believe it and therefore do not act according to it. This hurts our Heavenly Father very much and He expresses His dislike for it several times in His Word to us. Therefore, there is a great need for us to repent of this mistrust and change ways.

One of His most searing indictments of our hypocrisy in this matter is found in Ezekiel 29:13. "And they come unto thee (Ezekiel) as the people cometh, and they sit before thee as my people, and they hear My Words. But they will not do them, for with their mouth they show much love, but their heart goeth after their covetousness". Ezekiel describes us rather well! Covetousness seems to be our big problem. Isaiah 28:13 gives another reason why we honor Him with our lips without obeying Him. "Wherefore the Lord said, for as much as this people draw near me with their mouth, and with their lips do honor me, but have removed their heart far from me, and their fear toward me is taught by the precepts of men." I myself also have been taught wrongly that one should not fear the Lord but that it only means that we should be in awe about Him!

Indeed, many of our prayers are expressing our concern over the lack of things which we are supposed to need. Other prayers are often asking the Lord to fix our problems the way we think that they should be fixed. God's Word telling us that His ways are higher than our ways seem to have very little effect on our thinking! Many of the Lord's beautiful promises are connected to our trust in Him. Psalm 84:5 sums it all up. "Oh Lord of Hosts, blessed is the man that trusted in thee". It would be a very good thing if we all study God's Word, especially concerning our trust in Him.

We are created to give Him honor. Trust is one of the highest ways of doing this. We can worship and praise Him no better than to trust Him and while doing this, let the Holy Spirit convict our hearts by the words of Proverbs 3:3. "Trust in the Lord with all your heart and lean not unto thine own understanding". Proverbs 16:9 is a serious reminder to us that regardless our scheming, the Lord is the one who decides. "A man's heart deviseth his ways: but the Lord directs his steps". Do we really love and trust our Heavenly Father? Do we really know that ALL things work together for good to them that love God, who are called according to His purpose? (Romans 8:28) Even when disaster strikes? "The Lord redeemeth the soul of His servants: and none of them that trust in Him shall be desolate". (Psalm 34:22). Lord, help me to put my complete trust in You by knowing that You, my Heavenly Father, always knows best.

FAULTY THINKING

In order to come to some kind of system of Bible interpretation, some very well learned men have written books laying down rules of Bible translation call hermeneutics.

Although the study of hermeneutics can be very useful, you will soon discover that depending on which authors rule book you choose, you will get some different and sometimes conflicting rules.

One of the rules most of the hermeneutics teachers agree on is, when you read the Bible you have to take the then existing culture in consideration in order to have a better understanding. That seems to make sense, does it not?

The big problem is, however, if you are too uneducated to know what the existing culture was during the time of that particular writing, you are just out of favor to understand it correctly.

Another big problem is that more and more so-called bible-believing teachers are using the cultural argument to teach that because our cultural conditions are different from the time of Apostle Paul's writings, we do not have to obey some of his instructions. It comes down to that we must pick and choose which of God's instructions are for us today and which part of God's Word can be disregarded.

One writer has a clever way of terminology. He calls picking and choosing, "crossing the interpretive bridge when you read Paul's writings, which is needed to come to a right understanding".

Did God inspire His servants of old to write the Bible in order for us to disregard and nullify some of his instructions because they do not fit in our modern culture? Or course not! The very idea is ungodly absurd.

Especially the Pauline letters seem to be handled this way. Our Heavenly Father must have seen it coming that they would say "Oh, it is only Paul saying that". Because He reassures us that what Paul is saying is what He, God, is saying. (I Corinthians. 14-37) One of the worst violations of His Word is in regards to 1 Timothy 2:11-12. "I do not allow a woman to teach or to exercise authority over a man, but to remain quiet." But no, because the enlightened age we live in, where the woman is liberated and completely equal with a man in every way. We will and do ordain many women as elders and pastors. This is what this rebellious and so-called Bible-believing generation is saying! This regardless of several other instructions from God, concerning women in the church. (1 Timothy 2:11; 1 Timothy 3:2). Can you imagine an elder or pastor not having authority over the men in the congregation? Or how can a woman be the husband of one wife which is listed as a requirement for an elder.

Jesus' strongly worded warnings on nullifying God's Word by using our tradition and culture are mostly completely being ignored. Both in Matthew 15 and Mark 7, he condemns the then religious leaders. "Why do you also transgress the Word of God by your tradition?" "You are honoring God with your lips while your heart is far from me". "And many more such things you do". Surely the position of women in the church today is one of the plainest teachings in the New Testament! But our New Age enlightenment has mainly nullified God's Word. Even the terminology as man being the head of the household seems to be "political incorrect", all this with devastating results. There is a price to pay for disobedience. Why are traditions and culture so hard to change? Basically it seems to be the herd instinct in people. There is very little discernment by the average church goer because many are not "baptized with the Holy Spirit". Thus the attitude is "that is the way it has been for a long time and many others are accepting it". It must be ok. Take the tradition of following the Old Testament tithing doctrine for instance. Most protestant churches have followed the doctrine since the reformation. The leaders have been teaching it now for around 400 years! But the Lord has withheld his blessing on it because it is still one of the most disobeyed teachings in the church. According to reliable statistics, less than 2% of church members are giving the tithe. The Lord speaks in His Word of "words falling to the ground". (1 Samuel 3:19) This is exactly what is happening with the teaching of the tithing doctrine. The Lord is very displeased with it because he has given us new instructions for the new covenant. "Let every man give according to his own heart" (2 Corinthians 9:6). Of course, this stubbornness in disobedience might also be enhanced by the greed motivation factor. But even when the teacher's intentions are good and sincere, the Lord will not bless unbiblical teaching.

When you live in a small town consisting mainly of faculty and staff of a conservative Christian college and seminary, filled in by an ever changing student body, you will notice soon that unless you are a part of the religious education system, you are generally regarded as an uneducated outsider. This idea and trend is also working throughout national Christian churches. When they are seeking pastors, the major requirement is usually a degree from a cemetery . . . .(excuse me), seminary or a theological university. The famous and well known institutions are then preferred. Thus apparently such traditional religious education is considered to be the major qualification for spiritual leadership! What is even worse than this unbiblical trend is the more and more implicated idea that the ordinary uneducated person can not read and understand the Bible correctly by himself! This satanic idea, more and more followed by the Roman Catholic church from the dark and middle ages on, developed into completely forbidding the Bible for ordinary people and languages! This has had devastating results and most likely allowed many absurd unbiblical doctrines to develop. But today, much of the same trend is noticeable in the literature of the religious education establishment. Very low key and much of it by implication, the orthodox protestant leadership is now also saying the same. Unless you studied ancient cultures: Hebrew, Greek, Latin and hermeneutics, etc., one cannot interpret the Bible properly! This is a big lie, straight from Satan!

When you hear or read God's Word, the condition of your heart is the only condition the Lord looks for. Do you have a heart which loves God and is set and willing to obey when you hear? In the Old Testament, the Lord exhorts us many times to hear him. Most of the time the Hebrew word "shama" is used which means hearing with a discerning heart and a willingness to obey and declare. Would you dare to say that our Lord is only giving this ability to a privileged few, who went through our traditional religious educational system? Not according to what He tells us in His Word! In Mark 7, Jesus says "many more such things you do". We could mention many more examples also of God's Word being disobeyed, but there is already enough here to make God's point, "Honoring me with your lips, but you heart is far from me". Remember, Jesus is coming back very soon and to many religious leaders, he might say, "Depart from me, I do not know you". Let us hope and pray it will not be me or you, teacher!

FRIENDSHIP

Most of us value friendship very much. I certainly do and the Lord has given me several good friends during my life. However, do to the fact that I have traveled and relocated a lot since my wife, Clazina died, I seem to have difficulty lately to make new friends in my new location here in Virginia.

Last week I was using an old devotional booklet, the "Daily Bread", when I read a short devotional by Anne Cetas, titled "Good Buddy". For some reason, it touched my heart a great deal and I felt so comforted and happy when the Lord spoke to me through this devotion. He assured me that He was indeed "my Buddy".

The story was about a pastor's prayer in church. After he started his "Dear Heavenly Father", he was suddenly interrupted by an electronic voice from the organ, which said "Hey there, good buddy!" The congregation was awe-stricken and astounded and talked about this for a long time.

Mrs. Cetas points out that it is very biblical to consider the Lord as your friend and mentions Exodus 33:11, where God talks to Moses as a man talking to his friend. Also, Jesus himself declared us His friends if we obey His commands (John 15:14). As I reread John 15:10-19, the Lord spoke to me that I have not thought of Jesus especially as a friend. It suddenly dawned on me, that with a friend like Jesus, how can I be unhappy?

From now on, I hope to realize that He always is there, regardless where I relocate. He is my best "buddy" and always there to help me. Thank you Lord!

By writing this, I hope that some of you will be strengthened and encouraged also by this idea that Jesus is your friend always whenever you go, as long as you obey Him.

GOD'S SECRET AGENT

This is how I perceive the Holy Spirit, the third person of our triune God. I came to feel this way when the Holy Spirit talked to me in 1970, after I started addressing and worshipping Him. It was a rebuke, telling me not to continue to do that. God was displeased with it, although my motivation and heart was Godly.

When researching the subject, I found that not a single person in the New Testament ever directed himself to the Holy Spirit, neither in worship or prayer. In studying the Lord's introduction of the Holy Spirit, recorded in John 15:7-16, I concluded that the Holy Spirit is the Lord's working agent in the entire world and that He wanted to stay in the background himself, only revealing all things about Jesus, who had been given all authority by His Father. Jesus called him the Spirit of Truth, the Comforter and Counselor.

Now every time when I hear my fellow Christians addressing and inviting the Holy Spirit to come, it is as if I hear Him shouting "Do not you know that I am with you or in you all the time and that I am permeating the whole earth? In the unbelieving world, I am convicting of sin and revealing righteousness and judgment to others".

God is very displeased with this apparent unawareness of His omnipresence by His children and the Holy Spirit as a part of God and sovereign being everywhere. It does not behoove us to invite Him or tell Him that He is welcome. He even goes to places where He is not welcome!

Jesus declared that especially in believers, He is present all the time, either with them or inside of them (John 14:17). There are several scriptures telling us of His presence, saying that He never leaves us or forsakes us, that He wants us to have communion with him all the time, 24 hours a day (I Thess. 5:17), and that our bodies are the temple of the Holy Spirit (1 Cor. 6:19).

If you are one of the many Christians who are worshipping and inviting the Holy Spirit, please consider this writing as a message from the Lord and cease addressing the Holy Spirit.

SEVEN PRINCIPLES OF NEW TESTAMENT GIVING

Love is the essence of our Christian Faith. Love is a manifestation. It must be demonstrated in order to exist. "God so loved the world that He gave His only Son." (John 3:16) Therefore, giving is the primary expression and manifestation of love. God's Word says, "He who loves has fulfilled the commandments (law). All the Lord's commands are summed up in, "Love your neighbor as yourself" (Romans 13:8-10). In this light we have to see the whole subject of giving.

Jesus requires under the New Covenant that if we love God and are born again, that we give our all as a reasonable service (Romans 12:1-3). Here, we arrive at principle number one.

1. Give your all to the Lord. Defining the word "giving" in its totality, including all kinds of giving, you must be willing to offer 100%! As a Christian, your whole life belongs to Christ, including all your possessions, your wife and family, etc. "I beseech you therefore brethren, by the mercies of God, that you present your bodies a living sacrifice, holy, acceptable unto God, which is your reasonable service" (Romans 12:1).

2. Give as your heart directs you. Talking about the financial aspect of giving, God's Word says, "Let every man give according as he purposeth in his heart" (2 Corinthians 9:6-12). This gives us the foundation for understanding the Lord's will for our financial giving. This entails acting not upon the set rule of Old Testament tithing, but rather, obedience to the urging of the Spirit within the heart of each believer. This will likely result in greater generosity in giving than mere tithing. As it says in verses 6 and 7, "Now this I say, he which soweth sparingly shall reap also sparingly. And he which soweth bountifully shall reap also bountifully."

Now some biblical interpreters claim that this passage in 2 Corinthians is only speaking of special monetary gifts which were separate from the regular tithe. However, it is clear that such interpreters are wrong and that this passage actually rejects completely the Old Testament legalistic view of thinking.

3. Give willingly. In this same passage, we are commanded to give "not grudgingly or of necessity or under compulsion, for God loves a cheerful giver" (2 Corinthians 9:7). Now, this could go with giving 10% if this is what your heart directs you to do. Make sure, however, that it is not misguided teaching which compels you.

"Giving until it hurts" has become a popular refrain with many Bible teachers. Now, if this means that you, with a cheerful and glad heart, are denying yourself something in order to be able to give, this the Lord would love, because it would be following Christ's example. "Though he was rich, yet for your sake he became poor that you, through his poverty might become rich" (2 Corinthians 8:9). What great need there is today for Christians to live less sumptuous and more austere lives in order to bring the Gospel of Jesus!

4. *Give generously*. Another aspect of Christian giving is generosity. There are two main scriptures in which the Lord encourages us to be generous in our giving:

" . . . he which soweth sparingly shall also reap sparingly; and he which soweth bountifully shall reap also bountifully." (2 Corinthians 9:6)

"Give and it shall be given unto you; good measure, pressed down, and shaken together, and running over, shall men give into your bosom. For with the same measure that ye mete withal it shall be measured to you again" (Luke 6:38).

These exhortations are by no means an encouragement to give in order to get. This "give to get" teaching is very popular today, but it is also very un-biblical as it caters to our greed. They have a nice slogan for it and it sounds very spiritual. "Seed-faith giving" it is usually called, but it is still very ungodly. The only right motive for giving is love – self-denying love!

5. *Give regularly and proportionately*. "Now concerning the collection for the saints, as I have given order to the churches of Galatia, so do you also. On the first day of every week, let every one of you lay by him in store, as God has prospered him" (1 Corinthians 16:1-2).

Now, giving a set percentage is not what the Lord is thinking of here. Why not? He is looking at how much self-sacrifice is involved. How much did it cut into your basic needs? If the Internal Revenue Service realized that in order to have fairness of burden they need to have different brackets (percentages) for rich and poor, how much more is our heavenly Father looking for fairness of burden.

6. *Give without "tooting your horn" about it.* "He that giveth, let him do it with simplicity" (Romans 12:8). Some other translators use "without ostentation" (display). How different from the teaching in most modern churches. The use of pledges, envelopes and bookkeeping systems seems to run counter to what the Lord Jesus taught us in Matthew 6:3 "Let never your left hand know what your right hand is doing". "But we need tax receipts" you say. Do you really?

7. *Give out of what you have and not out of what you do not have.* The scriptures teach that " . . . . the gift is acceptable according to what one has, not according to what he does not have" (2 Corinthians 8:12). Therefore, avoid any kind of pledge drive or those incentives to give money called "faith promises". You can not and should not try to make deals with the Lord, setting conditions that when He is going to give you extra, then you will give it back to Him. It is subtle, but shouldn't we focus upon faithfulness to Him with what finances we already have rather than ask Him to somehow bless us with an unexpected extra sum of money (which costs us nothing in terms of labor or finances) which we will then turn over to Him?

Goodness and Mercy

In 1970, a team of Asbury college students, who were touched by the Holy Spirit, visited a church on the southern border of Georgia. That church was set on fire by the Holy Spirit also, and in turn, sent a team of young people to our church in Orlando, Florida. The same Holy Spirit fire came down upon our church and our entire family of five was greatly affected by it.

The Lord gave me a special promise scripture for my family to remember always. It was from Psalm 23:6, "Surely goodness and mercy shall follow me ALL the days of our lives: and I will dwell in the house of the Lord forever". We have been singing it ever since and we truly have experienced the reality of it.

The Lord's goodness and mercy has daily become very real to us. However, we had to discover that the Lord has a different and better idea of what His goodness and mercy is for us. It can and does sometimes include some very unpleasant and hard things for us like accidents, disasters, sickness and suffering.

At first, I did not understand this and I had to learn the hard way that "His ways are higher that our ways" (Isaiah 55:9). But then, slowly, we learned to trust Him and believe that "all things work together for the good to them that love God, to them who are called according to His purpose" (Romans 8:28).

Our four children are married and gone now. My wife of 54 years and I are close to entering the House of the Lord forever. Praise His holy Name! Gratitude and praise overflows our hearts. We are still making that melody in our hearts and devotions. Because our Lord is faithful and is doing what He has promised, so must we!

INTEGRITY

The Webster dictionary defines the word integrity as: "A firm adherence to a code of special moral conduct". What a wonderful good concept of a character trait this is! Does our Lord want us to have this trait? Does He want us to practice it? We better know that this is a big YES for sure!

Therefore, one would expect that Christians, who are followers of Christ, would show a great deal of this trait in their lives. But sadly enough, that does not seem to be the case. It is rather rare to find a person who has outstanding integrity and is a person on who you can rely on completely.

The King James Bible mentions the word "integrity" several times, but only in the Old Testament. Many Bible translations are using different words for it, like righteous, trustworthy, incorruption, soundness, etc. I like the word used in Psalm 7:8 the best of all, "The Lord shall judge the people; judge me, Oh Lord, according to my righteousness and according to my integrity". Here is integrity linked to righteousness!

In the NIV and RSV Bible the word integrity is also used in the New Testament. Titus 2:7 says, "In everything set them an example, by doing what is good. In your teaching, show integrity, seriousness." The King James uses here the word "uncorruptness". There are many other scriptures indicating that our Lord wants us to have integrity. To mention some: 1 Kings 9:4; Job 2:3, 9; Job 27:5 and Proverbs 20:7.

When Jesus was teaching not to swear, He was saying in Matthew 5:37, "Simply let your yes be yes and your no be no. Anything beyond this comes from the evil one!" Teaching with integrity means also that what you are teaching others you have to do yourself. Jesus rebuked the Pharisees strongly in Matthew 23:4, "for laying heavy burdens on their hearer, but not doing it themselves." He said "do as they said but not as they do".

Let each one of us really examine ourselves to see if we do show integrity. Let us ask the Lord daily for help to improve in this area. Are we Christians, people whom other people really can rely on? I find a good way for us to improve in this area is not to make impulsive promises too hasty when we see a need, but rather do it at once if that can be done, because we all seem to have the tendency to procrastinate or forget what we have promised and planned to do. Also, avoid announcing our future plans, because the Lord says we really do not know what tomorrow will bring (James 4:14).

FORSAKEN?

When our beloved Lord and Savior, Jesus Christ, cried out in agony on the cross, He used His heavenly prayer language, which was not understood by the onlookers. However, it was interpreted by the Holy Spirit in God's Word.

He cried out "Eloi, Eloi, lama sabachtani?" that is to say, "My God, my God, why hast thou forsaken me" (Matthew 27:46)? Although Jesus had foreknowledge of many things, His Father God had spared Him the foreknowledge of the awesome fact that He had to be forsaken temporarily.

Father God has used and is still using the picture of the human father/son relationship, so that we can have a more clear understanding what the Father went through, by not answering His beloved Son at this time. There have not been any moments in the world's history in which both our Heavenly Father and Son has suffered more intensely, than at that moment of Jesus' cry.

Can we really fathom the ultimate suffering of both our Father and His Son at this moment when the temporarily separation occurred? It should fill us with awe and sorrow, but at the same time with joy, knowing that it happened for us and our sins! Gratitude is flooding our hearts for this token of His tremendous love for us!

Thank you Lord!

SUPERNATURAL MIRACLES

One of Webster's definitions indicates that it does not always have to be supernatural but it can also be an "extremely outstanding and unusual event". This definition shows that for some people the word miracle not always means divine intervention which descents natural law. I always thought that the word miracle was used too loose by many people. What does God's Word say about miracles? One thing is for sure, our God is a miracle working God!. "They saw or see the miracles" (Deuteronomy 29:3, John 2:23). He even raises people from death!

We must keep in mind, however, that our Lord also allows Satan some miraculous powers sometimes (Exodus 7:11, Revelation 19:20). Therefore, when we hear about or see miracles, we need divine discernment to judge if it was a true miracle done by God.

From the Old Testament, it appears that our God wants us to know and remember the miracles He did for His people (Deuteronomy 11:3). From the New Testament, we learn that the Lord uses miracles often to approve of His messengers and the message. John 2:23, Acts 2:22, Acts 8:6 and Heb. 2:4—"many believed when they saw the miracles".

In John 6:26, Jesus rebuked people for the fact that they were not seeking Him for His miracles but for the bread, which they had seen Him produce. He was not rebuking them for looking for miracles, but for looking for material gains. Therefore, it is safe to say that the Lord is displeased if we ask for miracles to get material gain and many times you hear people asking for that.

Overall, I believe that it is not good for our faith to be looking for miracles all the time. The Lord has set in motion the natural laws of cause and effect and requires of us that we live by faith in His wisdom and love for us. He seems to overrule some natural laws sometimes, especially with divine healing of our bodies. But in many cases, He sets into motion our belief in healing powers, which He has created in every one of us. This is usually not immediately, but not less divine. I would not call this a miracle as such. However, absolute miraculous healings have been and still are being reported, even by the medical society. Praise His Holy Name!

Let us therefore trust completely in our loving and miracle-working God!

THY LOVING KINDNESS

The Bible, God's Word, mentions His loving kindness some thirty times. No wonder that when our family was baptized with the Holy Spirit in 1970, this particular expression became very significant to us. We started singing from scripture and especially sung Psalm 63:3-4: "Because Thy loving kindness is better than life, my lips shall praise Thee. Thus will I bless Thee while I live: I will lift up my hands in Thy name". Of course, you cannot sing this without lifting up your hands. However, at first, we did not lift our hands up very high. Many newcomers like us were flying them "half mast". But later on, we started to lift our hands as high as possible, even waving them to the Lord! Freedom in the Spirit was released! Kindness and to be kind is certainly of divine origin. Webster defines it as "being disposed to be helpful and solicitous". Indeed, the Lord's loving kindness is definitely connected to His deeds of help and His concern for our well-being. It is good to proclaim and tell about the loving kindness of the Lord, which you yourself do experience, because Isaiah 63:7 says "I will mention the loving kindness of the Lord" and on the end of the verse "according to the multitudes of His loving kindnesses." Psalm 25:6 is also speaking of

61

His loving kindnesses. Notice that it is mentioned in plural form here. This means that loving kindness is not only the attitude of the Lord but also His kind deeds because someone's attitude is not expressed in plural form. King David cries out in despair, apparently sick and depressed. Psalm 88:11 says "Shall Thy loving kindness be declared in the grave? Or Thy faithfulness in destruction"? Thus he is pleading to be healed and able to continue to declare the Lord's loving kindness. What also deserves notice is that God's Word mentions twice His loving kindness in the morning and Thy faithfulness every night." "Cause me to hear Thy loving kindness in the morning: for in Thee do I trust." Is it not wonderful to start your day with God's loving kindness? If we do that, another verse connects it to all day and the night. Psalm 42:8 says, "Yet the Lord will command His loving kindness in the day time and in the night. His song shall be with me and my prayer unto the God of my life". What a blessing it is to wake up sometimes during the night with a song and a prayer unto the Lord in your mind! Several other verses are connecting loving kindness to our human lives, starting to tell us that we need redemption and continuing to tell us that it draws us, resulting in His salvation through Jesus, finishing with our complete preservation. Psalm 103:4 speaks about it redeeming our lives from destruction. Jeremiah 31:3 speaks of it as "drawing us". Psalm 17:7 is telling us about salvation through His right hand. Psalm 40:1 is speaking about our preservation.

I am ending this devotion with my biblical reason for emailing it to you all: Psalm 40:10 – "I have not hid Thy righteousness with my heart. I have declared Thy faithfulness and Thy salvation: I have not concealed Thy loving kindness and Thy truth from the great congregation."

NEVERTHELESS

The word nevertheless is a very important word in the Word of God! God uses it many times to express His mercy and grace towards us, regardless of the fact that we do not measure up entirely to His standards. We all fall short!

I will use the marvelous fishing story of Luke 5:1-11 as an example what nevertheless combined with obedience can do. Here Peter uses the word "nevertheless" in verse 5: "nevertheless at thy Word I will let down the net."

What we see here are two phenomena. First of all, his lack of faith, caused by his own sound reasoning as an experienced fisherman. It seemed kind of useless to him to fish again because "we have tried in vain all night". Our own so-called sound mind often times interferes with what God wants us to do.

Secondly, his attitude of obedience to Jesus' command to "launch out in to the deep and let your nets down for a draught". This obedience was most likely the result of his love for Jesus. Do you love Jesus? Then you want to obey His commands. (John 15:14)

This marvelous story tells us of God's mercy, that even though we have very little faith, He will honor our obedience to His commands resulting in great blessings. This principle of a working little faith is also confirmed in God's Word by Matthew 17:20 and Luke 17:6 "if we have faith like a grain of mustard seed". Jesus was saying that then nothing shall be impossible for us. Take note however, that in the verse before (Luke 17:5), the disciples are admitting their lack of faith and asking the Lord to increase their faith. What God is telling us here is that if we confess our lack of faith and ask for help with an attitude of obedience, we will receive His unction.

Of course, the Bible also declares that "the just shall live by faith" (Romans 1:17) and "that without faith it is impossible to please God" (Hebrews 11:6). It is clear that it takes only a small portion of faith to receive His unction. In His great mercy He already accepts our mustard seed size of faith! Hallelujah! Praise His Holy Name! According to God's own Word in Mark 4:31, a grain of mustard seed is less than all seeds (very small and insignificant).

Another very significant place where Jesus used the word nevertheless, can be found in the three Gospels, where God records the suffering of His Son in the Garden of Gethsemane. Matthew 26:39, Mark 14:36 and Luke 22:42 talk about "nevertheless not as I will, but as Thou wilt". This is the ultimate example of obedience combined with the great mercy of God because *our Father was willing to give His only begotten Son for our salvation* (John 3:16).

In Psalm 89:19, I believe that God is speaking about Jesus, "His Holy One". In verse 30-32, it speaks about "His children" then in verse 33 is says "nevertheless my loving kindness will I not utterly take from Him, nor suffering my faithfulness to fail." Thank you Lord! His grace and mercy is covering our failures! Nevertheless, we should use this word in our prayers many times. "Lord, I am sinful and weak in faith, nevertheless . . . . ." If we tell our Heavenly Father this before we voice our desires and do it with a sincere heart, He will surely honor our requests.

THE NORMAL BIBLICAL CHURCH

If the Bible is our guide and handbook, we should follow the biblical example of how the New Testament Church was structured. To assume that we can do better by following our cultural traditions is very arrogant and has produced a sick church.

Most contemporary churches are following at least six unbiblical ways to structure themselves, mainly following cultural traditions as opposed to biblical examples. I will list them by number:

1. First of all, we can see that the early church never bought any real estate to build buildings in order to have their meetings. Although it seems that in the very beginning they used synagogues, but later on when that became impossible because of persecution, they met in houses and formed house churches. In the entire New Testament, there is not record of believers buying and building meeting places.

2. As far as the naming of the churches is concerned, we must observe the following: most likely in larger towns, there were several of these house churches, together forming the local church of . . . . (name of town). For further identification,

the name of the person in whose house the meetings where held was mentioned. The New Testament mentions always only the name of the town where the church is located. If we would follow this biblical example, the idea then would be reinforced that there is one body and that together we form the Body of Christ. Chasm and denominationalism would be greatly reduced and the concept of the "universal world-wide body" would be greatly enhanced.

3. The leadership structure which the Lord intended for the church to have is mainly summed up in the word "elders". He states that He has given to the church five different kinds of elders – apostles, prophets, evangelists, pastor and teachers. In conflict with today's practice, the title "pastor" is used only one time in the King James Version of the New Testament. The church is pictured as a theocracy and not a democratic organization. We must also take notice that there has to be multiple (elders) leadership. There is also no hint that there is a human head elder that has authority over the other elders. Jesus is the only head in the church. This implicates that the elders must exorcise their authority with unanimity. The old pyramid structure of command in the Old Testament is changed under the New Covenant in multiple leadership. Another important direction for the New Testament church is: but I do not permit a woman to teach or to have authority over a man, but to be in silence". For this reason, there cannot be any women leaders in the church; however, there is scripture to support women exercising the gift of prophecy in the church.

4. There is no scriptural support for the church conducting financial drives or pledge campaigns, neither for receipts and bookkeeping and budgets. A local church can receive financial help from other churches, but as a rule the ministry of a local church should be supported by

its members who are all "priests" in the ministry of love. Some specific rules for giving are:

a. "on the first day of the week, let each one of you lay aside something, as the Lord has prospered him, that there be no collections when I come."
b. so let each one give as he purposes in his heart not grudgingly or of necessity: for God loves a cheerful giver.
c. "For if there is a willing mind, it is accepted according to one has and not according to one does not have."
d. "But when you give to the needy, do not let your left hand know what your right hand is doing.

As far as salaries for the workers in concerned, the Bible does say that a worker is worthy his pay and that one should not muzzle an ox that is treading out the grain. However, the Lord does indicate that He prefers "tent-making" ministers who are providing for themselves.

5. The Lord also gives specific instructions as how to conduct the church meetings. The basis is "the Lord is a Spirit, He must be worshiped in spirit and truth" which means that we have to follow His instructions given to the Church in His Word.

a. "I will pray with the Spirit and I will also pray with the understanding. I will sing with the Spirit and I will also sing with the understanding."
b. "Whenever you come together, each of you has a psalm, has a teaching, has a revelation, has an interpretation."
c. "Is there anyone among you sick. Let him call for the elders of the church and let them pray over him anointing him with oil in the name of the Lord".

To sum it up, all the gifts of the Spirit should be in operation at one time or the other. When the Lord is truly worshipped, He will guide the congregation for all things that need to be done.

6. Regarding mission endeavor, the Bible shows how the first missionaries were sent out in the book of Acts. While the church elders at the church of Antioch were worshipping and fasting, the Holy Spirit guided them to send out Barnabas and Saul. There is no mention of any mission fund-raising campaign at that time or in the remaining parts of the New Testament. The missionaries were "tent-making ministers", providing for their own needs. Now and then they did receive financial help from other churches. There also is no precedent in the Word for the forming of mission agencies to oversee the missionaries to be sent. Mission was kept very simple and yet, it has been shown the most successful from the beginning. All the believers of today owe a debt to the early New Testament church, for their obedience to the leading of the Holy Spirit.

When we consider these six major departures from the biblical examples by the "modern" church of today, we should weep and repent and return at once to the guidance of God's Word. Or have we gone too far already and is it too late?

MOTIVATION

It is a must to always ask yourself "What is my motive for doing or not doing this". On the other hand, we should not judge another Christian brother's motivation. It needs to be established in your mind that the only major motivation of yours should be the first command of love, especially in obeying God's Word (John 15:14).

Notice that I used the word "major" in front of motivation. This is because it is common and natural that we have usually more than one reason. I was motivated to write this article because of two teachings I read from other Christian brothers and I feel that the Lord wants me to correct these wrong teachings.

The first one was teaching us that when we pray we should not be timid but bold and bind God to His Word. The second one was a brother teaching prayer and making the comparison with a 25 cent gumball machine. If you put your quarter of prayer in you get your delicious gumball for sure.

I know both teachings to be very wrong and displeasing to our sovereign Lord. First of all, you cannot and should not twist God's arm. It is good to quote God's Word in your prayers, but usually only His promises are quoted and not the conditions which are attached. Always we should add "Lord your will be done". This is not a cop-out or a lack of faith, but a proof of your submission to Him.

Secondly, God is not like a gumball machine that when you put your quarter in you get your gumball. You might get your gumball all right, but probably choke to death on it (Psalm 78:30-31)!

So why and how should you pray to God? I want and should do it because I love Him very much and want to commune with Him. Flowing out from this are obedience, needs, wants and knowing that He is our only source. Be aware that Paul is saying that love should be without "dissimulation" (Romans 12:9). This means sincere and without ulterior motives.

Now-a-days we hear a lot of evangelization basically saying "save your soul". If saving your soul is your major motivation, you are off to a wrong start already. The basic command is still repent and obey God in baptism. Your love for God is then showing in your obedience. The result will be that He will save your soul. Your salvation is the result of your love and repentance and never should be your primary goal.

I brought this out in my article "Purpose and Result" a while ago. This article is still available if you want it.

It is true that when you are a baby Christian, in the beginning you are restrained many times from sinning because of the fear of God and the consequences of your sin. However, you should become mature enough so that you can say with 1 John 5:3 "your commands are not grievous to me". You obey because your prime motivation is love. That all of you may be in this stage is my prayer.

OBEDIENCE

Obedience is absolutely essential in our Christian life. The Bible declares it to be the proof of our love for God (John 14:15). During my ministry in the Philippines, I learned to say this verse in the Llacano language at the beginning of my evangelism, because the Lord laid on my heart that obedience was what the new converts needed to start practicing in their lives. The first commandment states that we are to love the Lord our God with our entire being and our neighbor as ourselves. It will fulfill all other commandments.

When we love the Lord with all our heart, we not only want to obey Him because of the fear of the Lord (Deuteronomy 5:9), but also because we want to please Him (1 John 3:22). Also, although there are many blessings as a result of our obedience (Exodus 19:15), it should not be our prime motive.

Several years ago, I wrote an article on "Trust and Obey". It is still on my BlogSpot. I explained that the word "peculiar" in Exodus 19:5 meant set apart by God, different from the world. This is what happens when we obey God.

Should we be obedient to only a part of the New Testament? I say "New Testament" because many laws of the Old Testament are outdated by the New Covenant. I did explain that in my booklet titled "Our Precious New Covenant", which I have available free for anybody who wants it. Of course, James 2:10 tells us that we are supposed to obey all of the New Testament. Some people accuse me of being legalistic, but legalism is when teachers want to force the Old Testament laws on people. James 2:10 connects obedience with the "Law of Liberty".

The results of obedience are numerous and divine trust in God is one of them. Isaiah 50:10 mentions both obey and trust in one verse linked together. The fact that I feel prompted to write an article on obedience is caused by me meeting several persons lately who want to worship the Lord with their cap or hat on their head. Although they know 1 Corinthians 11:4, they seem to think that it is a less important issue that can be ignored! While God clearly is saying that every man who covers his head while praying or prophesying dishonors his head, I wonder, are they not concerned about this? Do they love wearing their caps more than loving their God? If you think that you can be unfaithful in these small things, know that Luke 16:10 tells us that then you will be unfaithful in the important things also!

The head covering is not the only issue in the Bible about which some people feel that it can be ignored by doing their own thing. I have met several people who are disregarding several other scriptures. The writings of St. Paul, especially, seem to be subject to disobedience. Take for instance, the issue of hair (1 Corinthians 11:14) or women's apparel and authority (1 Timothy 2:9-11).

Disobedience to God's Word comes with a very heavy price and that is becoming more and more evident in these last days in which we are living. Look at the increase upheaval in the world! Some people are using the Bible itself to excuse their disobedience. Quoting 2 Corinthians 3:6, "The letter killed but the Spirit gives life." It does not say that the New Testament rules are killing us! Would the Holy Spirit contradict God's Word and tell us you may disobey and ignore 1 Corinthians 11:14? No way, Hose!

Some others accuse me of majoring in the minors! Well, as far as minors are concerned, in the light of obedience to God's Word, there are no such minors!

It is my prayer that this article will cause you all to obey God's Word more and more and in doing so will be very much blessed.

ETERNAL SECURITY

This is the way most believers in "once saved, always saved" prefer to call this doctrine because it already sounds more spiritual. When you examine that doctrine, it really comes down to that once you are born again and saved, you can never loose your salvation. The purpose of this article is to show you that this is absolute wrong, unbiblical and dangerous thinking.

Eternal security is talking about eternal life with Jesus Christ after we are born again and it is the foundation stone of our Christian faith. We can have that during our life because even then we are "seated with Christ in heavenly places". But there is a lifetime journey to travel and a battle to be fought during which we have the great privilege to be sustained by our Lord. As long as we are in Christ, we do have this eternal security. God is very faithful! However, there is no biblical evidence that we cannot go wayward and therefore loose our salvation.

All scriptures talking about our security during our walk with God are mentioning, most of the time, the condition to be righteous or good. For example, in Psalm 55:22, it mentions that the righteous shall never be moved. Psalm 112:5-6 tells us that a good and righteous man shall never be moved. It is very true that our Lord in His great mercy will do an awful lot to prevent a Christian to fall away in perdition. I have experienced that myself during my teenage years. However, there can come a time that God gives up on you, when you are persisting that you will no longer follow Jesus and there by fall into great sin.

There are several warnings in God's Word, indicating that there is a possibility to fall away from the faith. The most direct one is in 1 Corinthians 10:12, "take heed lest they fall". Hebrews 10:26-31 is absolutely clear that a born again Christian can loose His eternal life! "When he is treading under foot the Son of God and has counted the blood of the covenant where with He *was sanctified* an unholy thing" (verse 29). There is then no longer a cure for your condition.

Hebrews 6:4-6 is also very plain about this. When you crucify the Son of God afresh and put Him to an open shame, there is no more cure. People who are sticking to the once saved always saved doctrine usually argue "Ach, they were probably not saved in the first place", when they are faced with the facts that some Christians in their circle went apostate. This is an obvious cop-out, however and is contrary to Hebrews 6 and Hebrews 10. Notice the word *was* in Hebrews 10:29 and the word *were* in Hebrews 6:4.

Let us make sure that we all heed the warnings in God's Word. A great comfort is to know that God does not tempt us beyond our endurance, but always makes a way to escape (1 Corinthians 10:12-15). Verse 15 says "I speak as to wise men, judge ye what I say".

THE GOOD SAMARITAN

This parable from Jesus is found in Luke 10:29-37. It was the answer of Jesus to a question from a lawyer who wanted to justify himself. The question was, "Who is my neighbor?"

The question itself is very legitimate because we can understand that God is not just talking about the people who are living next door.

In the light of the fact that daily there are so many urgent needs presented to us, we need to make choices as to whom we apply our aid. All of us have limited resources and abilities. Other than prayer, we cannot attend to the sufferings of the whole world. Therefore, it is good to know from God which neighbor we should help.

From this parable, we can deduct that our God will place those who need help on our pathway and it might even be people we do not like very much! There was a great dislike between the Jews and the Samaritans! Jesus showed also that being a member of the clergy does not make you necessarily more spiritual.

Besides answering the question who our neighbor is, the parable also paints a picture of Jesus Himself. He is the Good Samaritan. He was also rejected and despised. The traveler was probably a backslider because he was traveling in the wrong direction. He was not going up to Zion, the City of God, but returning to Jericho, the easy place of entry into the Promised Land. (I am assuming here that you have heard that the journey of God's chosen people to the Promised Land is a picture of our Christian life.)

When we are going the wrong way, our merciful God does many things to prevent us from backsliding and going into perdition. In this case, the highway robbers got to the traveler. The Good Samaritan (Jesus) was the only one who had compassion and took the wounded traveler back to the inn (the church). He did this after applying wine (God's Word) and oil (the Holy Spirit). Before he left, he paid a down payment for the cost and promised to return to pay in full.

Hallelujah! Jesus is coming back and will pay in full for our complete restoration! Let us praise and worship Him!

PLEASING GOD

To please our Father God is an essential thing to do for a Christian. Jesus is our example in addition to being our Lord and Savior. Therefore, we should always do those things that please Him. 1 Thessolonains 4:1 states that we are beseeched and exhorted to walk and please God in order for us to abound more! The NIV Bible says in the last part of Ephesians 5:10 "find out what pleases God". Of course, when we love God, it is a natural outflow of our love. It is still necessary for us to know which things will please our God and we should research and find out God's Word on it and then practice it. This article aims to help you with your own research.

Hebrews 11:15 refers to Enoch, who was raptured when he pleased God. The Lord found it so important for us to know this that He referred to Enoch three more times in His Word (Genesis 5:18, Luke 3:27 and Jude 14). I believe that in order for us to be included in the future rapture, we also need to be pleasing to God! There are many verses telling us what pleases God. In Isaiah 56:4 we find that while speaking to the eunuchs, God said "keeping the Sabbath and choosing the things that please me". (Please study my first article on our day of rest). Here are some more verses about pleasing God: Philippians 4:18 – "a sweet smelling sacrifice (gift)"; Colossians 3:20 – "obey your parents in all things"; 1 Corinthians 1:21 – "through foolishness what was preached to save, God was pleased". Here are some verses to look up for yourselves: Psalm 69:32, 135:3, 147:1, Proverbs 15:26 and 16:7. Our Father God also states several times what displeases Him! Romans 8:8 "they that are in the flesh cannot please God" and "without faith it is impossible to please God (Hebrews 11:6). Numbers 11 is talking about people who are complaining and Psalm 2:5 tells us that people who plot against His anointed "He will vex them". Some more verses are Isaiah 59:15, Ezekiel 33:1, Zechariah 1:2-15, Mark 10:14 and Hebrews 10:27. God also tells us what He hates! Divorce is one of the rebukes (Malachi 2:14-16). Yet the divorce rate among Christians is slightly higher than average! Another word of rebuke to some churches today can be found in John 12:43, Thessalonians 2:4, Ephesians 6:6, Colossians 3:22 and Galatians 1:10. It is telling us that we should do things as pleasing to God and not to men!

Many churches today and especially in the large mega churches do everything to please and attract people. I found some indication of that in a very popular book "The Purpose Driven Church". Of course, their sincere desire I hope) is to attract more people for Christ's sake. However, a good goal never justifies worldly methods. I wonder what kind of Christians is being produced. Pleasure and entertainment seekers, maybe? After ending with this controversy, I hope that you are stirred up enough to start researching for yourselves and respond to me with some commentary. That you all may please God is my prayer.

HANNAH'S PRAYER

I want to share with you one of the most remarkable prayers in the Old Testament, a prayer of thanksgiving and praise by the mother of Samuel, through which the Lord gives a detailed revelation of Himself. A barren woman named Hannah had received an answer to her prayer for a child and pours her hear out in ten short verses (1 Samuel 2:1-10).

The remarkable part is that the Lord uses her prayer to reveal a great deal of His being to us. He did this by putting it in His Word. It established without any doubt His total sovereignty, autonomy and power over His creation. A message we are in need to hear very much today because so much false teaching on our authority, healing and prosperity has eroded our belief in God's complete sovereignty.

I will attempt to give Hannah's prayer here in a free translation in order to make it clear what God is saying about Himself:

Verse 1. She starts her prayer with acknowledging God and giving Him credit for lifting up her strength and opening her mouth.

Verse 2. Testifying that God is the only true God and establishing His holiness and steadfastness.

Verse 3. Warning against pride and arrogance. God knows all and He is the one who decides and judges.

Verse 4. He humbles the mighty and strong, but helps the stumbling weak.

Verse 5. The rich well fed become poor and in want, but the hungry poor are fed by God. The barren women become fruitful but the fruitful women with several children will become weak and depressed.

Verse 6. The Lord kills and gives life.

Verse 7. The Lord makes some men poor and others rich. He lifts some up and cuts others down.

Verse 8. God raises the poor out of the ash heap and gives them places of honor. He will have them inherit thrones in Heaven with the noble. He is in complete control of the earth (pillars) and is the Creator of all.

Verse 9. God will protect and guide the feet of His Saints but the wicked will be silenced and perishing in darkness. No one will prevail by his own strength.

Verse 10. God will break his adversaries into pieces, thundering against them from heaven. He will judge all people on the earth. Gives strength to his King (Jesus) and exalts the power of His anointed one (Jesus). Amen.

Hallelujah for the Lord God Almighty reigns! Let us rejoice and be glad and give the glory until Him!

PREDESTINATION

This doctrine has been controversial for a long time. It seems that Calvin was one of the first I know of who tried to vocalize this doctrine. The controversy about this doctrine has caused great damage to the relationship between Christians in the churches. Lately, a book by David Hunt titled "What Love is this?" has denounced Calvinism as heretical and thereby hurting many people. This is very unfortunate to say the least. It shows to me that there is a great misunderstanding about this biblical word "predestined". Therefore, I would like to state what I believe is the true biblical meaning of this word.

God has predestined all of mankind to have eternal life with Him. The four verses which mention this word are: Romans 8:29-30 and Ephesians 1:5, 11. All of these verses are talking about being destined to eternal life. Well, the argument goes that apostle Paul is writing to the saints in Rome and Ephesus and therefore it was meant only for them or maybe for existing Christians only. That may or may not be true, but does that mean that God has predestined all the others to hell fire? Of course not! One cannot find that in the Bible.

One of the reasons for misunderstanding the issue of predestination, I believe, is the fact that most people do not take into consideration that our God has complete fore-knowledge and is totally timeless. These are things we humans cannot grasp with our finite minds. For God, in His spiritual realm, no time exists. For Him, the past is the present and future and vice versa. However, His Word does indicate that He wanted to have eternal fellowship with mankind from the beginning of His creation, but apparently He did not want to program us as puppets or robots, but wanted that men would obey His commands voluntarily. Here is where men's so-called free will comes in. I said "so-called" because this term is actually a misnomer in my opinion. It causes people to believe that they actually can choose whatever they like, without God being able to interfere and that is not true!

Throughout God's Word, He keeps calling people to repentance and the word "whosoever" in John 3:16 means that salvation is available to everybody. God also says that when we were yet sinners, Christ died for us (Romans 5:8). Also, we as Christians cannot claim to have chosen Him, because Jesus clearly stated in John 15:16 "you have not chosen me but I have chosen you". We only have to choose and decide to respond to His invitation. This does mean that we have the ability to reject Him but even when we do reject Him initially, He will keep calling us to repentance for a while. There are numerous divine calls to repentance in God's Word – Jeremiah 33:15, Ezekiel 33:11, Hosea 6:1, Matthew 22:3, Luke 14:17, Revelation 3:20. Of course, there is a moment in our Lords timing that He will allow you to go with Satan into hell fire, but this always will be the persons own choice! Therefore, our only choice is to respond to his invitations.

Out of the wrong thinking about predestination has come the idea that some people are born with a body which is bound to keep doing perverted things. I am referring here to many modern scientists, who are telling us that they discovered that certain perversions like homosexuality, kleptomania (stealing) and several other perverse addictions are born into some people. So therefore many homosexuals, for instance, are claiming now that they are doing their natural thing and cannot help it because God made them that way! This, even though the Bible clearly condemns the homosexual practice. It also tells us that we always remain fully accountable for our yielding to temptations.

1 Corinthians 10:13 says that He always will provide a way to escape temptation and that He will not "suffer" you to be tempted beyond your endurance.

Although it is a biblical fact that we are all born in sin and that our natural tendency is to sin against God, the Bible tells us that we do not have to remain that way. Our loving Heavenly Father has provided a way out. Through belief in Jesus Christ, His Son, we can become "new creatures" and then sin shall not have dominion over us (Romans 6:9-12). God wants everyone to come to repentance and become destined to eternal life with Him through faith in Jesus Christ. That it may be so for all of you is my sincere prayer.

THE PRECIOUS PROMISES OF OUR LORD

The devotional booklet "Our Daily Bread" has a title for the devotion of May 25 called *Frustrating Promises.* It starts with the question, "Do any Bible promises frustrate you?"

I must admit that in the past I was many times frustrated and probably there are many Christians today who are frustrated, asking themselves, "Why don't I have what I want?" I believe that our main problem is the fact that we do not ask according to God's will and are ignoring the conditions for the fulfillment of the promises.

In the first place, most promises are for "the righteous man". Therefore, we must know what it means to be a righteous man. According to the New Covenant, a righteous person is some one who is washed clean from his sin by the blood of Jesus, confessing by faith that Jesus died and has risen as our Lord and Savior. James 2:20 tells us also that our faith has to be a living faith, manifested by good works.

Psalm 37 has indeed, many precious promises; however, it gives us also 17 conditions and instructions how to be doing "good works". I will list them here verse by verse:

Verse 1 – "Fret not thyself" (also in verses 7 and 8)

Verse 3 – "Trust in the Lord and do good" (also verse 5)

Verse 4 – "Delight thyself in the Lord"

Verse 5 – "Commit thine way into the Lord"

Verse 7 – "Rest in the Lord and wait patiently for Him"

Verse 8 – "Cease from anger and forsake wrath"

Verse 9 – "The meek shall inherit the earth"

Verse 21 – "The righteous show mercy and give"

Verse 23 – "A good man"

Verse 26 – "He is ever merciful and lendeth"

Verse 27 – "Depart from evil"

Verse 30 – "Their mouth speaks wisdom, his tongue talketh of judgment"

Verse 31 – "The law of his God is in his heart"

Verse 34 – "Wait on the Lord and keep His way"

I count seventeen conditions for the promises of Psalm 37. They form the Lord's definition of a righteous person and "good works". In verse 39, He again tells us that it is for "the righteous".

When we do not see the promises of the Lord happening in our lives, we should examine and ask ourselves, "Where do I fall short and how can it be corrected"? If you know the answer, ask the Lord for help in this matter. That is certainly a prayer according to His will and He will answer that (1 John 5:14).

PERVERSION

"It is becoming increasingly clear that much truth that has been held about homosexuals is less scriptural and theological-founded than we first believed!" This statement is written by Pastor Piazza of the Cathedral of Hope Church, who claims to be the largest homosexual church in the world. This is written in a six page leaflet on homosexuality as an introduction. He continues to state that discovering "the truth" is relatively recent. What he actually seems to say is that the poor, dumb people who have not caught on to this recent truth have been and still are reading the Bible wrong!

Let me say this from the onset. *It is impossible for Christian homosexuality to exist!* It is a misnomer, because the two worlds are contradicting each other. A practicing homosexual can never be a Christian and the Bible states that. The deed itself is condemned by God and eliminates the chance for a homosexual to inherit the Kingdom of God (1 Corinthians 6:9-10). God says "Know ye not that the unrighteous shall not inherit the Kingdom of God." Then our Lord says "be not deceived"!

Then our Lord starts listing who the unrighteous are: fornicators, adulterers, effeminate or abusers of themselves with mankind. Continuing in verse 10: "nor thieves, nor covetous, nor drunkards, nor revilers, nor extortionists shall enter the Kingdom of God". This is clear enough not to be deceived by believing that a practicing homosexual can be a Christian! However, at the same time, it continues to say in verse 11, "as were some of you", indicating that overcoming it by repentance and the blood of Jesus, it can be forgiven, but they have to change.

What Mr. Piazza is doing is encouraging homosexuality and this is leading his sheep to hell! He also denies that a homosexual person can change. He is quoting a report of six cases of conversion and he says at least four of them went back to their old "lifestyle". The reason for this is that God created them like that when they were born, so their reasoning is that for this reason God does not condemn them.

Again, Mr. Piazza is saying that this new idea is just a recent discovery because we modern people know and understand so much more now! The leaflet continues to say that because Jesus never said anything against homosexuality, he was not against it! What an ungodly conclusion! Mr. Piazza even suggests that the Gospels might have been referring to "homo" people. They take the case of the Roman Centurion, who was pleading Jesus to heal his servant. He had an unusually intense love for his servant and therefore, it could have been a "homo" relationship! How far can one go and how deep one can sink to prove something! Another far conclusion is reached on Jesus' teaching about eunuchs (Matthew 19:10). Jesus said that some are born as eunuchs and Mr. Piazza says he must have been talking about "homos" and lesbians.

To do away with Leviticus 18 and 20, he reminds us that the old laws are not applicable any longer for today and therefore homosexuals are ok. He also deals with New

Testament scriptures and it all sounds very spiritual. He mentions Romans 1:18-32 in which Paul speaks strongly against homosexual sin. But according to Mr. Piazza, Paul was only referring to "homo's" temple prostitution and was definitely not referring to same sex love! Paul clearly had no concept of persons for whom this kind of "lifestyle" is natural. Poor Apostle Paul, he had it all wrong anyway!

In 1 Timothy 1:8-12, Paul lists again a group of wicked people, among which are "homos" and calls them ungodly. However, Mr. Piazza states that there is a mistranslation of the term effeminate and abusers of themselves with mankind. We understand it wrong by thinking that it was talking about people of "same sex orientation". Mr. Piazzo also treats the Sodom story as if homosexuals were not involved. It is too bad that through the ages we have called "homo's sodomites! According to Piazzo, the men involved in Sodom were not "homos". Because Lot offered them his daughters! Also, if the Sodomites were "homos, God did not have to destroy them because they would die out by themselves since they were childless. Mr. Piazzo's conclusion is that the Sodom story cannot be used as an argument against "homos".

My conclusion about this ungodly perversion is different. A. The gay people are completely perverted, besides their actions, their mind is also perverted. They cannot think logically and clearly anymore. B. The main reason for that is found in Romans 1:24-25. "Therefore God gave them over in the sinful desires of their hearts to sexual impurity for degrading of their bodies with one another". Verse 25: "They exchanged the truth of God for a lie." C. They are doing that by accusing God of creating them as homos.

We, who are opposed to this perversion, are called "homophobic". This is a new word created by their enlightened world. They also stole and misused the word "gay". I take the label "homophobist" with honor and pleasure, knowing that our Lord is pleased with us. I hope and pray that He is also pleased with you my friend because you also make a stand against the perversion of homosexuality.

THE PRIESTHOOD OF ALL BELIEVERS

This concept of the "Priesthood of all Believers" has been completely disregarded by the Roman Catholic Church. Not until the reformation has this doctrine been practiced by the Protestant Churches. Even now, the Roman Catholic Church remains very much opposed to this concept. They still follow the Old Testament system of priestly hierarchy and have a ranking system for their priest, ending up with the Pope on the top.

The New Testament does not support this hierarchy system, but nevertheless, some of this is still found in the Protestant churches of today. The New Testament clearly teaches the idea that Jesus is the only mediator and high priest and all believers belong to the "royal priesthood" (1 Peter 2:5). Several other verses imply this idea that the Lord considers us to be His priest for now and in the future millennium (Romans 12:4-9, Hebrews 13:15, Revelation 1:5, 5:10, 20:6). The word clergy is not mentioned in the Bible.

The great commission is for all believers, of course, and the Bible says nowhere that only the clergy can baptize and serve communion or serve as ministers to other people.

The opposite is true. (See Romans 12:4-9, where several ministries are mentioned and all to be done by believers.)

Sadly enough, most Protestant churches have fallen back into clericalism, where pastors do almost the entire ministry. This to the great hurt of the Universal Church. It has produced many believers, who are only bench-sitters and who have never ministered or brought another soul to Christ.

Many pastors are ignoring the 5-fold ministry, which God has ordained for the church. (See 1 Corinthians 12:28 and Ephesians 4:11.) In my opinion, this is causing the latter day apostasy, of which 2 Thessalonians 2:3 is speaking about to develop.

It is my hope and prayer that none of you will become apostate but keep enduring until the end. Jesus is coming soon friends! "Even so Lord Jesus, come!"

PROPHECY

Prophecy is a gift from God and according to God's Word, prophecy has a three-fold purpose, "but he who prophecies speaks edification, exhortation and comfort to men." (1 Corinthians 14:3) Prophets are so important to God that He gives prophets to the church, together with apostles, evangelists and pastors and teachers. (1 Corinthians 12:28 and Ephesians 4:11) It is not hard to understand why, when we look at the deeper meaning of these three purposes.

Edification: literately building up in holiness. Exhortation means giving strong advice or warning, urge strongly, incite or encourage. Comfort: to console, reduce grief with the purpose to encourage. Hallelujah, what a great need there is for these three purposes of prophecy today!

Remarkable, although the Lord Himself appoints prophets in the Body of Christ, He encourages every believer to qualify for the job by learning! First of all, He tells us that He wants us ALL to prophecy (1 Corinthians 14:1-5). Then in 1 Corinthians 14:30-31, He tells that we can all prophecy one by one so that we may learn! This to the extent of the fact that the "regular" prophets have to give the new learners a chance to learn!

The concept of learning involves making mistakes at first. My conclusion therefore is that we should not judge the beginning prophets too harshly for some mistakes, although verse 29 tells us to judge prophecy. Harshly judging and condemning has been part of the reasons why there are so few saints who attempt to prophecy. The evil one is trying with great success to prevent prophesying by corrupting it and making the people afraid to learn it. How sad this is! Our Lord must abhor this!

Some preachers are saying that actually their preaching is prophesying. Although I do admit that preaching the Word has to involve also the three purposes for prophecy, I find the context of what the Lord is saying in 1 Corinthians 12 and 14 about prophecy not in line with the concept of preaching. What the Word says about preaching is different.

Personally I have notices that beginning prophets (including myself) sometimes did start off in the Spirit speaking for God but then going astray by adding something in "the flesh". A gentle correction by other mature saints is in place. We have to judge prophecy but not prevent or stop it. John 4:1 says that we have to test the Spirits, whether they are of God "because many false prophets have gone out into the world".

New Testament teaching about prophecy does not tell us to stone the false prophets to death if their predictions do not come true. I believe that is because since Jesus went to heaven and we are living in the age of Grace until He comes back to judge us. It also seems that New Testament prophecy is not so much about telling the future as the old prophets often did. He is giving the new prophets grace for a chance to learn.

The Lord has given us a plumb line to judge by. The plumb line is God's Word itself as recorded in the Bible.

If it edifies, exhorts and comforts and is in line with the Bible, you may assume that it is from God. Thirteen years ago when we returned from the Philippines, I received a prophecy for the church and I spoke it out in a congregation. Ever since then I felt that the Lord wanted me to repeat it to as many believers as possible. So here follows a part of the prophecy I did give:

"My children, you are living in the last days. And today, the deception I am warning for in My Word is taking place world-wide. My sheep are being led astray by much false teaching. If it were possible, the very elect will be deceived, unless I cut the days short. I want to give you a straight plumb line to measure all the teachings of today by. Does what you hear center in on Me and My Word and thus give Me glory and pleasure, says the Lord? Or is the teaching and doctrine centered and focused on man and his comfort? Apply this plumb line says the Lord. Then you will not be deceived and then you shall endure until the end. Thus says the Lord."

So let us not despise prophecies, but let us test all things and hold fast what is good (1 Thessalonians 5:20-21).

Purpose and Results

Revelation 4:11 is one of the several verses in God's Word in which He reveals the reason why He created us. It states, "Thou are worthy, Oh Lord, to receive glory and honor and power; for Thou hast created all things and for thy pleasure they are and were created". One can say therefore, that unless we fulfill God's purpose for our existence, we miss the boat entirely, so to speak.

Humanism of today says essentially that our goal should be the happiness of mankind. However, it is very sad that not only unbelievers believe that this is so. This kind of thinking has crept into Christianity also. Even so-called evangelicals and fundamentalists are preaching that eternal life and all the other divine benefits are our main goal. Repent and have eternal life is commonly preached everywhere. Therefore, many people become Christians to save their own skin, so to speak. What is happening is that we are confusing the results of becoming a Christian with the purpose of our lives, which our Lord has set, which is *to bring glory to God.*

It is true, of course, that God's Word, the Bible, is telling us a lot about the results of repentance and becoming a Christian. However, all these benefits should not be our primary goal! When we make the benefits of our repentance and salvation the goal, then the self-love in our lives can be reigning and even hinder our prime purpose for being. We encourage our self-centeredness and putting the cart before the horse by making the resulting benefits our main goal.

How can we glorify, honor and please God? Primarily by being obedient to God's Word. There is no better way to honor and glorify God than to accept His total superiority and obey His Word. His first demand is that we repent from our sin and believe in Jesus Christ, His Son, who washes us clean from sin with His shed blood. Then Jesus affirms that our primary command is to love God and our neighbor as He has loved us. In John 15:14, He states, "If you love me, you keep my commands". Obedience is the total key for our Christian life.

I want to formulate here in seven simple points, the essence of the Gospel and what God's Word tells us about fulfilling the purpose of our lives.

1. First of all, there needs to be a willingness to obey and fulfill the purpose of our lives. (Isaiah 1:19)
2. The only way we can start pleasing God is by accepting Jesus Christ, His Son, and having the shed blood of Jesus cleanse us from our sins. Then we will be able to obey the first command of loving Him and our neighbor.
3. At the moment of our repentance, we are born again and become new creatures, children of our Father God. The Holy Spirit, who brought us to this point, will be with us.
4. The proof of our love is obeying Jesus (John 15:14) which will result in a Godly life, full of the divine

benefits God has for his children. We will worship the Lord and magnify His name all the time.

5. After being baptized in water in obedience and as proof to the other believers, we seek the baptism with the Holy Spirit (John 7:37-39). The Holy Spirit will come in us to empower us to witness (John 14:17 and Acts 1:8).

6. The Holy Spirit will daily sanctify us and change us into the likeness of Jesus. Until the end, when He changes us completely, in the twinkling of an eye, to have eternal life with Him (1 Corinthians 15:52).

7. We abide in the vine (Jesus) during our Christian life and will bear much fruit that way (John 15:5). This will result in much glory to God (John 15:8).

Let us make sure that all these things are taking place in our lives because our pleasure is not the main purpose but it is God's pleasure with us.

QUESTIONING GOD

Already this title gives the believer the sense that even this concept of questioning God is not proper. But I must confess that I myself have been doing that during several happenings in my life. I did not always have the feeling that the Lord did not like it, although sometimes I was rebuked for questioning Him.

To go farther than this, I believe that sometimes the Lord wants us to ask "why", because He has given us a message through certain occurrences in our lives and He wants us to learn something from it. To find out what the Bible is saying about our questioning Him, I have researched the Scriptures and found that there are actually two kinds of our human "whys".

The first kind, which God sometimes answers, comes from an earnest desire from us to know why certain things are happening in order to learn from it and improve into the likeness of Jesus. There are not many examples of this kind of "why" in the Bible, but there are some very significant ones.

In Genesis 25:22, Rebecca, who is pregnant with Esau and Jacob, is questioning the Lord, "Why I am thus?" In verse 23, He gives her an answer, telling her in fact that the elder (Esau) will serve the younger (Jacob). Amazingly, the Lord finds it so important for us to realize His total sovereignty that He uses this to mention this again in Romans 9:14-24. "Jacob I have loved by Esau I have hated". The Lord explains His displeasure about the clay asking the Potter "Why hast Thou made me thus?"

Another good example of an apparent righteous why question is from Moses in Exodus 32:11. He is asking God why He is so very angry and continues to plead for His mercy. This is followed by God's mysterious statement in the King James Version, Exodus 32:14, "The Lord repented from the evil He thought to do unto His people!"

The best righteous "why" question in the New Testament is by Jesus Himself, "Eli, Eli, lama sabachtani, My God, My God, why hast Thou forsaken me?" (Matthew 27:46 and Mark 15:35) Father God's answer is found in most of the New Testament and especially in John 3:16. His great love for us is the reason!

The second type of our "why" is really a sign of our rebellion and disagreement with what God did or is doing. We really dislike what is happening and do not understand that our God will work His good for all of us who believe in His Son. We usually think that we know what is best, but God tells us that His thoughts are much higher and different from ours. In Romans 8:24, He states "All things work for the good to those who love God and are called according to His purpose."

I believe that most of us have been guilty of this wrong attitude in asking "why". I must confess that I have been guilty of this on several times in the past when painful and unpleasant things were happening. The last time was in 2004, when Clazina, my precious wife of fifty-five years died from cancer. For several weeks, I could not see the good of that and complained to the Lord, asking "Why".

But He has mercy and has given me peace with it and forgiveness for my rebellion.

Several years ago, when I was already retired, we attended a Full Gospel Church. One day, the main sanctuary burned down. To my great dismay, the leadership and most of the members seemed to avoid the question why this had happened. Most of them seemed to say that it was just providence and something that happens normally while others blamed the devil for it! They refused to consider that the Lord might have a message of displeasure with them and did not learn their lesson.

A good example of the Lord's displeasure with a wrong kind of "why" question is found in Numbers 11:20 when the Israelites were complaining about the lack of meat and asking "why came we forth out of Egypt?" The result was the plague with the wrath of the Lord came while the meat was still in-between their teeth.

I surely hope that this writing will help you all to avoid the question "why Lord" with a wrong disapproval attitude and we must also accept that sometimes the Lord remains quiet upon our questions. It is His prerogative.

SABBATH:
THE LORD'S DAY OF REST

Usually when I feel the need to write about a Christian subject, it is because of something which happened and stirred me, so here is the story behind this article:

There was a wonderful, Godly congregation of believers in a small town. They were interdenominational and blessed with nice roomy facilities. They had a great zeal for world-wide evangelism. Their young Godly pastor led them in very nice praise and worship services. He loved His Lord very much and was totally inclined to obey His Word. Of course, when a church is doing so good, it becomes a primary target for Satan.

I can imagine that Satan had a conference in His realm and asked "How can we best break this congregation up?" The demons decided to do it, in this case, through the confrontational doctrine of Sabbath-keeping! They managed to convince the pastor, through books and other people, they had to honor and use Saturday as the Lord's Day, rather than Sundays. He proposed to change the worship services to Saturday. It is not hard to imagine what happened next!

A division among the people developed quickly. The leadership of it was a relative elder. They had several meetings, but the issue could not be resolved, so our Pastor resigned and now the former pastor and the opposition elder are accusing each other of causing all of the damage to the church. Although I do not know what exactly happened in their meetings, the young pastor started this controversy and was used by Satan to break up this church! It is my prayer that this article will prevent many more schisms Satan is planning.

First of all, we should know that the beginning of the naming of days cannot be precisely determined. Some believe it occurred around the time of the Tower of Babel because they were aware of seven of our nine heavenly bodies, the sun, moon, and the five other planets. Later on, a little before Christ, the Roman Empire started using Latin names for the seven days. They got intermingled with Saxon and Nordic heathen concepts. This is what developed: Sunday – Sun; Monday – Moon; Tuesday – Tewe's Day (a Norse female deity); Wednesday – Wooden's Day (teutonoc theology. It was before called Mercury's Day from which comes Mecredi); Thursday – Thors Day (the god of lightening); Friday – Frigg's Day – a rotund Germanic female deity. It use to be Venus Day (Vendredi); Saturday – Saturn.

The Jewish people go as far back to the days of Moses and the giving of the Law. Before this, the entire world had gone through great periods of spiritual darkness (Noah's flood and the Tower of Babel). Most likely no days were known.

In addition to this, I do not believe, on the basis of the Genesis creation account, that the Lord is talking about our 24-hour day periods, because during the first three days, there was not even a sun and moon, which sets our

24 hour day! Even if they picked the correct so-called seventh day, there is the fact that God's Word tells us that He turned back the sun at least two times! One time ten degrees on the sundial and during another occasion, He lengthen day six with at least half (2 Kings 20:11 and Joshua 10:13-15)!

I point this all out to make sure that you understand that it is impossible to know for sure which day was the original day the Lord our God rested! So how foolish it is to fight and debate about what is the seventh day. One thing we should know. It is very important to God that we keep one day as rest and holy. Here we give the devil a foothold. Since Constantine, around 300AD, the world system gave its approval to Sunday, keeping as the day of rest. But most people had no concept about our Lord's desire to keep it holy. It deteriorated almost at once in a day of leisure and pleasure. Even today, many church-going Christians spent most Sundays on their own pleasure. In Isaiah 58:13, God lists several things not to do on the Sabbath: Not doing our own pleasures and going our own ways, not even speaking our own words! How much watered down is our Sunday rest today? This is still a great failure of the Church today!

Apparently, our Lord saw this controversy coming and put in His New Testament some warnings, not to judge one another concerning food, drink and keeping of holy days and Sabbaths. Romans 14:5-10 tells us clearly that people can esteem different days of the week and in Colossians 2:16 it says "Let no man judge you in meat or drink or in respect of any Holy day or of the new moon festival, or of the Sabbath days!" Legalism was already a problem in the New Testament church. Some wanted to keep the circumcision and the Sabbath-keeping.

Does all this mean that the Lord did not leave us any indication as to what day the early church used? Of course not! To let us know which day became the Lord's day of rest, when they were meeting and breaking bread together, He mentioned the first day of the week (Acts 20:7). Also, the collection of the Saints listed in 1 Corinthians 15:2 was ordered on the first day of the week! The Lord does not tell us some things for nothing! When Paul uses the Synagogue on the Sabbath, it is every time, in order to find converts. In my opinion, based on all of this, the early church felt a great need to set them apart from Judaism and chose the first day as celebration of the Lord's resurrection. Because it is God's Word, it shows His approval of it. In 1 Timothy 4, God tells us that all things which He created are good by our prayers and praise. Praise His Holy name for our Sunday!

Do you love our Lord? Then please Him with a day of rest and devotion and do not use it to split any part of the Body of Christ.

Our Biblical Sanctification

God's Word mentions the words sanctification, sanctified and sanctify many times. In the Old Testament it is mentioned more than 100 times and in the New Testament more than thirty times. Jesus himself mentions it four times, three of which are found in His prayer for us in John 17. Therefore, there is no doubt that the Lord wants us to know and understand this doctrine of sanctification. I am sure that Satan recognizes the importance of this doctrine, because He seems to exhort a lot of effort in order to distort it and make it ineffective to the believer. I am referring here to the wrong doctrine of ENTIRE sanctification, which some denominations and evangelical Christians seem to hold. They add the word "entire" on the basis of mainly one verse, which is actually a salutation on the end of the first epistle to the Thessalonians. 1 Thessalonians 5:23 states "Now may the God of peace Himself SANCTIFY YOU WHOLLY and may your whole Spirit, Soul and Body be preserved blameless at the coming of our Lord, Jesus Christ". Although this verse shows that there is such a thing as being sanctified wholly, or as you will, entirely, it shows that this entire sanctification will not take place until the coming of the Lord Jesus Christ. When I read this scripture, as I remember maybe sixty two years ago, I understood it as Paul's salutation and blessings actually meaning to express his desire that they were going to make until the end. This understanding has been confirmed the rest of my life by studying God's Word and the conformation by the Holy Spirit. By adding this word "entire" to the doctrine of sanctification, the evil one is creating a lot of confusion, double-talk and pride in many Christians. He does that by suggesting that we can lead a complete sinless life. That fills us with guilt when we find that we cannot obtain it or with pride when we imagine that we are perfect sinless already. So let us take a good look at Biblical sanctification. The word "sanctification" (from the Greek word "Hagiasmos") according to Webster means "The state of growing in divine grace as result of Christian commitment, after baptism or conversion". The verb "sanctify" (hagiazo) means "set apart for a sacred purpose". The word "saint" comes from the Greek word Hagios. These are very good definitions underwritten by God's Word. The complete picture, which the New Testament gives, is that sanctification is both an instantaneous happening at conversion and an ongoing drawn out process, which comes to completion "in the twinkling of an eye" when Jesus takes us at our death or at the time of our rapture. At our true conversion to Jesus Christ, we all become Saints and the Bible calls us so (1 Corinthians 1-2 and Romans 1:7). This is accomplished by Jesus shedding His blood and dying on the cross for us to wash away our sins and from then on God looks at us as forgiven saints. There is no Biblical support for the idea that we actually reach a complete sinless state during our life. However, our sins are continually forgiven because when we remain in Jesus, He makes intercession for us with the Father. Besides Jesus Christ Himself, there never has been and never will be a human who is perfectly sinless. God's Word teaches us that "there is no one who does not sin" (2 Chronicles 6:36 and "there is not a just man on earth that does good and does not sin" (Ecclesiastes 7:20). Apostle Paul states in Romans that we all are falling short and in Philippians 3, he declares that he has not already been perfected. If Paul had not reached that perfect state yet, who are we that we should claim that we have or even that we can obtain that state?

We are exhorted by the Word to continually pray for forgiveness of our sin. It would be useless if we did not commit any sins anymore, would it not? That sanctification is a life long process is made clear by God's Word. For instance, in Hebrews 10:14 says, "for by one offering (Christ death on the cross) He has perfected those who are *being sanctified*". Being sanctified by the Holy Spirit is also used in Romans 15:16 and it clearly indicates an on-going process. I must indicate that that process can be interrupted by us. The Lord's stern warnings ring out loud and clear in Hebrews 10:29. "We are worthy of much more punishment, if we trample the Son of God under foot, counting the blood of the Covenant (Jesus blood) by *which He was sanctified*, a common thing". From verse 26 to verse 29, the Lord gives the most severe warnings to us. It is awesome and very direct language. I recommend for all Christians to read this over and over because although we are new creatures in Christ and have HIS promise that He will hold us, we remain prone to sin. Those sincere Christians, who are reading into God's Word that one can lead a complete sinless life, are coming to a very erroneous and dangerous conclusion. It has shown to lead to all kinds of wrong interpretation of the Word. A president of a conservative Christian college wrote me one time that they were holding the view that the doctrine of entire sanctification was just another wording for the baptism with the Holy Spirit! I think he did not realize that he rejected this event for today and the terminology that Jesus himself used for it. It also seems that they get fortified in the wrong thinking about sanctification by misreading scriptures about Christian perfection and holiness. The writings of John Wesley on Christian perfection especially seem to have confused many Wesleyans although I think that Wesley did not go so far as to say that we can lead a sinless life and that he or anyone else was completely sinless. However, other writers in the past and contemporary have gone through great effort to explain away the Scriptures which are saying that there are no sinless human beings on earth. The word "perfect" comes from several different Hebrew and Greek words used in the Bible. It shows how complex this concept is. In English, it can and is translated sometimes with mature, completed, finished and improved. The way I see the word "perfect", is that the Bible shows that only God is perfect and that Jesus was the only one who had lead a perfect life. That has to make the word "perfect" rather relative to us. The Bible shows us in different states of perfection: babes, children, young people, adults and elders. Therefore, I believe that when we are in that stage of Christian life, in which our Lord has led us, we can be perfect at that level. In other words, a person who is born anew in Christ is perfect at the level our Lord has brought him and there is no difference between a babe in Christ and an elder or vice versa. Each human being, in a class at a certain level, is not better or higher-rated than any other. When a person is reborn, he is a new creature and made perfect by the blood of Jesus. The Holy Spirit will grow him or her into more maturity until he/she is called up. That is why the Lord is not unfair in demanding from us, when He said in Matthew 5:48 for us to be perfect. In

2 Timothy 3:17, it says that the man of God may be perfect (complete) thoroughly equipped for every good work. He also commands us "to be Holy, even as I am Holy says the Lord". He knows we can be holy and perfect as long as we remain in His son Jesus Christ and are covered by His blood. In Him we are perfect and holy!

THE SOVEREIGNTY OF GOD

"Know therefore this day and consider it in thine heart that the Lord is God in heaven above and upon the earth beneath: there is none else". (Deuteronomy 4:39). This is just one of many scriptures in which the Lord is telling us that He is totally sovereign and completely in charge and in control of everything that is happening on this planet and in all of His creation.

In Deuteronomy 32:39, God declares "See now that I, even I am He and there is no god with me: I kill and I make alive; I wound and I heal; neither is there any that can deliver out of my hand." From this and several other verses like Isaiah 45:7, we can get the sure impression that our God wants us to know that He is doing it all.

From beginning to end, the Bible is full of verses which are speaking of the Lord's total power and sovereignty. Therefore, it is hard to understand why so many believers keep denying the Lord's doings in their lives! One of the reasons seems to be the wrong application of "men's free-will doctrine".

It is true that the Lord has given mankind the opportunity to choose Joshua 24:15 and Deuteronomy 30:19). Choose Him and between right and wrong. However, the Word also makes clear that with this opportunity to choose, He still remains in charge and control. Many times the Word shows that He keeps pulling the strings, so to speak. He does it in all kinds and different ways. It is good to look up some of these scriptures: His eyes upon them (Ezra 5:5), sending an evil spirit (Judges 9:23), harden their hearts or spirits (Exodus 14:4 and Deuteronomy 2:30), stirring them up (Cyprus) (1 Chronicles 5:26 and 2 Chronicles 36:22), turning kings hearts (Proverbs 21:1).

Especially the remarkable story in 1 Kings 22:22-23 and 2 Chronicles 18:21-22 is lifting up part of the veil hiding to us what is going on in the Lord's spiritual realm. It shows clearly that He even uses evil spirits sometimes to accomplish His will with men although He gave them power to choose.

The term "men's free will" seems to be a misnomer in the light of these revelations from the Lord. Although He said "choose you this day", many times He seems to steer and direct our will and actions. However, He does it in a way so that we humans remain accountable and responsible for our deeds.

The parable of the potter and the clay (Jeremiah 18:6) and also Romans 9:15-21 makes it very clear that He does what He wills and we cannot say "Why hast thou made me thus?" Verse 16 of Romans 9 sums it all up. Speaking of us humans, He says "So it is not of him that willeth, nor of him that runneth but of God that sheweth mercy".

As far as Satan is concerned and his power over humans, we must realize that Satan is completely subject to God's will. He can do only what our Heavenly Father allows him to do. The two prime examples of this are found in Job and in the saying of Jesus concerning Peter (Luke 22:31). In both cases, Satan had to get permission to do harm.

God's Word assures us that we the righteous, are in the Lord's hands (Ecclesiastics 9:1), although we must see to it that Satan does not have anything in us (John 14:30). The only way for us to be in that state is to be washed clean of sin by the blood of Jesus. Therefore, it is of primary importance that we believe and ask the Lord for forgiveness all the time. Only then, Satan has "nothing in us".

As far as our salvation is concerned, the doctrine of predestination is very difficult to understand and seems to bring a lot of controversy. The most important thing for us to know and remember is that it is the ultimate desire of our Heavenly Father that all of mankind will be saved. There are several indications of that in God's Word. For instance, the word "whosoever" in John 3:16 indicates that Christ died for everybody. But there are conditions attached to our salvation. The first one: we have to believe in Jesus.

Many people are not willing to fulfill the conditions and therefore were not and are not going to be saved. In that sense, God has not chosen them. The Lord is the one who does the choosing. There are many scriptures indicating this. One of the most well known, declared by Jesus himself in John 15:16 is "You have not chosen me, but I have chosen you". But we, as being chosen, have to respond to His love and believe in Him.

In the light of us having a choice, the biblical doctrine of predestination is hard to understand with our carnal mind. However, we are not required to understand it, only to believe and accept it. Ephesians 1:4-12 is very clear, it even states that before the foundation of the earth was laid, our Father has chosen us. The total foreknowledge of God is impossible for us to grasp. It has to do with

God's timelessness. In His spiritual realm, there is no time, meaning no past, present or future as we know it. This is an impossible concept to our human mind and causes many useless debates, but we must believe and accept God's Word. It will stand forever!

THE SOWER

The Parable of the Sower is so important to Father God that He put it three times in the New Testament, almost word for word. He wants to make sure that we, His human creation, will get the message. What is that first most important message? I believe that it is the fact that He expects us to bear fruit, reproduce and multiply!

He is using the agricultural picture of a seed being sown, reproducing and multiplying. We can find this parable in Matthew 13:3-10, Mark 4:3-10 and finally in Luke 8:5-9. A remarkable fact is that Jesus very seldom gives an explanation of His parables, but He surely did it for the parable of the Sower. In all three books, Matthew, Mark and Luke, the parable is followed by an explanation!

I will print here the parable listed in Mark 4: Verse 3 begins "Listen! A farmer went out to sow his seed. As he was scattering the seed, some fell along the path, and the birds came and ate it up. Some fell on rocky places, where it did not have much soil. It sprang up quickly, because the soil was shallow. But when the sun came up the plants were scorched, and withered because they had no root. Other seed fell among thorns, which grew up and choked the plants, so that they did not bear grain. Still other seed fell on good soil. It came up, grew and produced a crop, multiplying thirty, sixty, or even a hundred times. Then Jesus said, "He who has ears to hear, let him hear".

What we should also notice from this parable is that our Father God is dividing all human-kind into four categories. First, the ones that have hardened their hearts so much by trampling on the seed so that it lays there for the birds to pick it up! A garden or field has most always pathways, where the people walk to get to the part they want to work. On those walkways, the soil becomes too hard for the seed to penetrate. That is the picture Jesus is painting of people who trample on their conscience all the time, so they become unresponsive to God's Word. I found the word trample in Luke 8:5. I sure hope and pray that you do not belong to this group of people!

Secondly, Jesus pictures people here who are very worldly and shallow, very little depth of soil for the seed to shoot roots in. When times of testing, trouble or persecution starts, they quickly backslide after initially having received God's Word with joy! How sad. It is sure from this text that testing of your faith and trouble will start after accepting God's Word. Even persecution "because of the Word" can possibly follow. The Bible teaches us to be steadfast in our faith.

Thirdly—the seed which fell among the thorns. Here, Jesus tells us what the thorns represent in our Christian lives. Matthew states "the worries of life and the deceitfulness of wealth". Mark adds also "the desire for other things" while Luke also mentions worldly "pleasures". Who does not experience those trials and temptations? We all have to overcome them with the help of the power from the Holy Spirit. If we do fail here, we get choked and become unfruitful. It is my experience that sadly enough, many Christians do not heed this warning and fall for the temptations of the "evil one" who does not want to see many more people becoming followers of Christ, because this is what the fourth category implies.

Fourthly—the good soil. It requires listening to God's Word with an open and obedient heart and getting baptized with the Holy Spirit, who will help you to remove the rocks and the thorns. Then you will produce a crop, some thirty, some sixty and some a hundred-fold. That is the multiplication our Heavenly Father is after in this world!

Biblical fruit is pointing mainly to reproduction and multiplication. Because of our carnality, we think of it mainly as some goods for consumption. However, even the fruits of the Holy Spirit in Galatians 5:22 are there for helping us to reproduce other Christians. This comes out also in John 15 where the Lord gives us a serious warning that unfruitful branches will be burned. Do you really want to bring glory to God? The Bible teaches us that it is the main purpose for which we were created! John 15:8 tells us that bearing "much fruit" will bring glory to God.

SO LET US ASK GOD'S HELP AND START BEARING FRUIT!

THE SPIRIT OF GOD

In the Old Testament, the Spirit of God is mainly known by the Hebrew word "Ruwach". Starting with creating, he is already mentioned in Genesis 1:2. From the start he is the working agent of God. This is what I called him in my article "The Secret Agent of God". Although, in the Old Testament he is not as yet presented as the third person in the Trinity, progressively he is revealed, coming to the final revelation in the New Testament that he is the third person of the Godhead.

I have already written several articles on the Holy Spirit. There was "God's Secret Agent", "The Baptism with the Holy Spirit" and the "Promise of the Father". However, in view of the apparent lack of understanding by many people and the great importance of this doctrine, I feel led to write some more on this subject. This is probably because my family and I have experienced the baptism with the Holy Spirit with great effect on our spiritual lives.

The Old Testament mentions the Spirit of God (Ruwach) about 235 times, but the term Holy Spirit is used only twice, in Psalm 51 and Isaiah 63. The New Testament mentions the word "Pneuma" as Spirit between seventy and eighty times and it indicated "wind", the wind of God. The word Holy Ghost or Spirit is used some 340 times!

We should especially pay attention to what Jesus is saying because He had the Holy Ghost in Him, which He said was the Father in him. Notice first of all, he tells us we would receive the Holy Spirit when we are thirsty and come to him (John 7:37-39), this after He had been glorified. Then shortly before He was crucified, He explains the essence of the Holy Spirit and gives him a new name "the Comforter" (Parakletes), which the Father will give, to abide forever (John 14:16).

In verse 17, Jesus also calls him the Spirit of Truth. What escapes many readers is that Jesus is pointing out two different dimensions (volume, intensities) of the Holy Spirit. *With them and in them! With them now and in them later*! That there are different volumes of the Holy Spirit is underwritten by His parable of the Ten Virgins. Five had enough and five had an insufficient amount of oil (Holy Spirit).

In John 14:25, Jesus repeats the promised sending of the Holy Spirit, who will teach them all things and make them remember all things which Jesus has said. This is repeated again in John 15:26. In chapter 16, Jesus continues to explain the Holy Spirit who only will come when He goes away. Verses 7-15 are a detailed listing of who the Holy Spirit is and what he will do.

From this, we can deduct that the Holy Spirit does not seek to be worshipped by himself apart from the Trinity. Jesus pictures him as God's working agent who always reveals Jesus. There, the New Testament does not show any worship or prayer directed to the Holy Spirit. You should not worship or pray to him or direct yourself to him and invite him. He is not a gentleman who never will offend you or force you, as I have heard preach a couple of times!

You also do not invite the master of the house to come in. This is a type of arrogance and inappropriate. He will go everywhere he wants and convicts the world of sin!

The question therefore is, how do we receive this precious baptism with the Holy Spirit? Jesus spent His last breath on this world to tell us about it in Acts 8 and then read what happened in Acts 2. He told us to be thirsty and come to Him. Are you thirsty enough to obey? Do you have a strong desire to have more of the Holy Spirit? Is it evident by power evangelism in your life?

What we have today is a church with many members who seem to be satisfied with their powerless evangelism, not realizing that they are lacking the promise of the Father, as Jesus called it. They are in the situation of the people of Samaria in Acts 8, where is says "the Holy Spirit had not yet fallen upon any of them (Acts 8:16). Hopefully this is only temporary for you.

Are you satisfied with having the Holy Spirit with you instead of in you? The Old Testament pointed in Joel 2:29 to the outpouring of the Holy Spirit and Peter is referring to it in Acts 2:38-39. It would happen "afterwards". If it was afterwards when Peter spoke, how far we must be now into the last days! Act now, there is not much time left. What power would be to evangelize the whole world if every believer received the baptism with the Holy Spirit! Oh Lord, help us!

SUBMISSION AND REBELLION

God's Word clearly teaches us that we should submit ourselves to God (James 4:7). As believers, we should submit ourselves also to one another (2 Peter 5:5) and in addition, to "every ordinance of men" (1Peter 2:13). This however, only as it is not against the commands of our Lord (Acts 4:19).

I do encounter often other believers who are also saying that the Bible is the true Word of God and gives us correct guidance. However, they seem to object many times as to what the Bible is actually saying. There is much difference of opinion, even on major doctrinal points and this causes much disunity in the church. It shows to me that there is something very wrong with our thinking, that difference of opinions on major issues is a natural phenomenon and does not matter too much.

The Bible itself, however, is given us many exhortations to be like-minded and that seems to be completely ignored! (Romans 15:5-6, and 2 Corinthians 13:11) In Philippians, chapters one, two, three and four, we mostly seem to have the attitude that it is ok to have different viewpoints on scripture. That is not what the Bible says!

It causes great disunity and strife. The cure for this is found in Romans 8:6. It says that we have to be SPIRITUALLY MINDED! THEN IT WOULD BRING LIFE AND PEACE. But we usually manifest our carnal mind and verse 7 continues to state that this is enmity against God and cannot be subject to God's law. If indeed we would manifest to have the mind of Christ (1 Corinthians 2:16), we would be in unity, submitting to God's Word. We have to walk continually in the Spirit and not in the flesh.

I continually meet believers who are objecting to the common understanding of Bible verses, while claiming that they believe that God's Word is without error. It appears that our carnal mind is always looking for reasons not to submit to certain Bible teachings. I have heard many reasons from believers why they do not submit to what the Bible actually says. One of the major ones is "oh, but this is open to interpretation and my understanding is, etc., etc." Their usually preset opinion causes them to look for excuses not to accept what the Word really says.

I am going to list the three major excuses that are being used in order not to submit to certain Bible teachings.

The first excuse is "You have to take the culture of Bible times into consideration. At that time it meant something different". It was for then and not for now. Also because of mistranslation, you have to know the original Hebrew and Greek language.

The second excuse I hear often is "We cannot take this literally." One has to spiritualize this. The words cannot mean want they mean today. With this, they spiritualize almost everything that does not fit in their thinking.

The third excuse often used, even by scholars is "only parts of the Bible are didactic (with intention to teach). Some is only historic and not to be followed!" One scholastic writer even claimed that most of the book of Acts was only historic, implying that we do not have to follow the ways of the early New Testament church!

I will biblically argue against these three excuses here now:

1. I consider it totally absurd that our Lord has given us His Word so that only very learned people can understand it. The Bible is for everyone, including all the common, unlearned people. The only thing needed for our understanding is the inspiration of the Holy Spirit and the Holy Spirit is with every believer!

2. One of the main rules of sound hermeneutics is to take scripture literally as much as possible and only spiritually when it is very obviously required by applying our common Holy Spirit-guided sense. Most people, who have off-beat views on scripture, usually spiritualize everything that does not comply with their ideas.

3. To teach that only part of the Bible is didactic is going directly against God's Word of 2 Timothy 3:16, "All Scripture is given by inspiration of God and is profitable for doctrine, for reproof, for correction, for instruction in righteousness".

Not to submit what God is actually saying is rebellion against God. God compares rebellion with the sin of witchcraft!! This is very serious!

Dear friends, there is a great need that every one of us believers rebuke and correct this wrong thinking.

SUFFERING

The Word of God tells us a lot about this subject. Specifically, in 1 Peter chapters 2-5, we can find the clear teaching that we as Christians are "called to suffer" (1 Peter 2:21). It speaks of two kinds of suffering. First: The suffering for Christ's sake, meaning persecution and reproach, because of our faith in Christ. Secondly, the suffering because of our sins and the need for correction. Sickness is a major part of this second kind of suffering, although sin is not always the cause of our sickness.

The book of Job makes that very clear. Job was not stricken because he had sinned, but because God wanted to prove his loyalty and righteousness and allowed Satan to put sickness on Job. The Bible calls suffering for well-doing "better" than suffering for evil-doing. (1 Peter 3:17) This implies that all suffering is good for us.

We are admonished in 1 Peter 4:15 not to suffer for being an evil-doer and called happy when we are reproached for the name of Christ (1 Peter 4:14). We are also told that afflictions are common to all brethren worldwide and that after you have suffered "awhile", God will establish us firm and strong" (1 Peter 5:9-10).

That sickness is a major part of our afflictions and suffering is an undeniable fact. Paul mentions this kind of suffering in Colossians 1:24, where he is speaking of "the afflictions of Christ in my flesh". Most likely, he was speaking of the thorn in his flesh which was given to him (2 Corinthians 12:7). We should realize that our Father God chastises His sons every time there is a need for it (Hebrews 12:7). His purpose is to purify us and make us more Christ-like. Many times He seems to use sicknesses and finances as His major tools to accomplish this. In Hebrews 12:11, He makes the statement that "it seems grievous", but then assures us that afterwards it will yield "the peaceable fruit of righteousness". Therefore, in a sense, this kind of suffering can also be considered for "Christ's sake and His glory".

Jesus learned obedience by suffering according to Hebrews 5:18. How much more are we in need to learn this obedience? Although, many of our sicknesses are self-induced by mistreating our bodies, for Christians, it is still our Lord at work to purify us. When Satan is used, he has to be allowed by our Father God to afflict us. We are encouraged to endure, even to be happy and rejoicing when we are suffering, much against our human nature. However, it seems that the Lord allows us "to sorrow" about sickness (Philippians 2:27) but we should remain steadfast by believing in our Father's everlasting mercy.

We know that all things work for the good of those who love God and are called according to His purpose (Romans 8:28). Know also that if we suffer, we shall also reign with Him (2 Timothy 2:12).

THE THIEF IN THE NIGHT

This biblical expression of Jesus, concerning His return, has become widely known. Ironically however, although Jesus meant it as a warning to the world, the world has not accepted it. The general idea even among Christians: Well, Jesus will come unexpectedly, so there is no use for expectancy.

It is true that Jesus declared that the day and the hour of His return are only known by Father God (Matthew 24:36 and Mark 13:32) and therefore we should dismiss all prophesies and predictions about the day of His return. However, God's Word is very clear that the concept of His coming as a thief in the night is not applicable for Christian followers of Jesus when the Bible declares it! 1 Thessalonians 5:2 says that we perfectly know that the day of the Lord comes as a thief in the night and it continues to say in verse 4 that it does not apply to us as "the Brethren".

We Christians should not be asleep, but be watchful and sober (1 Thessalonians 5:6). The message right now from God is Romans 13:11, *"And that knowing the time, that now it is high time to wake out of sleep: for now is our salvation nearer than we believed"*.

The New Testament is full of exhortations to watch and wait for the Lord's return. It is called "our Blessed Hope" (Titus 2:13). 1 John 3:3 says *"and every man that has this Hope purifies himself, even as he is pure"* and according to Hebrews 6:19, *"it is an anchor for our soul"*.

We are also supposed to be ready to give an answer to every man that asked you about the reason why this Hope is in you (1 Peter 3:15). We can and should discern the times! Many events are indicating that everything is falling into place for the day of the Lord to take place soon. The parable of the fig tree is repeated three times in the Bible. The Lord says in Luke 12:56, expressing His frustration, "You Hippocrates, you can discern the face of the sky and of the earth, but how is it that you do not discern this time?"

Right now the time is very late; the Lord is coming very soon! I am close to eighty years old, but expect the Lord's return during my lifetime. Can we use the word "imminent"? If that word means right now, at once, as some people are saying, I do not think so. Some things still have to take place. But those could happen very quickly. Of course, thinking about our own death, which equals for us to be in the Lord's presence can happen at any moment! So we need to be ready, watching and waiting. The New Testament Church did this as an example for us. *"And now little children, abide in Him; that when He shall appear we may have confidence and not be ashamed before Him at His coming"*.

TENACITY

Although this word tenacity is not in the King James Bible, it describes the concept of steadfastness. One of Webster's definitions is "not easily pulled apart". God's Word makes it very clear that God Himself has this attribute in the greatest way and likes to see it also in His children. Therefore, the purpose of this article is to encourage you to develop and show this character trait.

Another English word, which appears only one time in the King James New Testament, is "perseverance". Ephesians 6:18 talks about persistent prayer with supplication (humbleness). Overall, this subject of tenacity is used many times in the Bible under different words like steadfastness, stand or hold fast, endure, continue, etc.

I want to focus in on the concept of enduring because it is mentioned so many times and links tenacity with suffering and hardship. Webster states the following definition: "to remain firm under suffering, hardship and misfortune, without yielding".

There is no doubt about the fact that Christians also have to suffer in this world and Philippians 1:29 states, "For unto you it is given in behalf of Christ, not only to believe on Him, but also to suffer for His sake". "Is given" sound to me that it is considered to be a privilege to suffer.

To live the Christian life is not a bed of roses. Our Heavenly Father will chastise us in order that we will grow more into the likeness of His son Jesus Christ (Hebrews 12:5-11). In verse 7, it states that God expects us to endure. When we follow a desire that God planted in our hearts, but experience suffering, most of the times God is testing and developing our tenacity. He wants us to have some starch.

However, when we follow our own desire without consulting Him, we also will surely suffer tribulations. It then means that the Lord is trying to stop us. In that case, our so-called tenacity is actually sinful stubbornness and the result will be extended tribulations.

If you do experience sufferings, tribulations and chastisements or hardships, ask yourself and God if you are following your own fleshly desire, which are not given by God. The required action then is to stop at once. But if your heart's desires are Godly and given to you by God, no matter how much and what kind of hardship and sufferings you endure, obey 1 Corinthians 15:58, "Be ye steadfast, unmovable, always abounding in the work of the Lord. For as much as ye know that your labor is not in vain in the Lord".

Matthew 24:13 says "But he that endures until the end shall be saved". Beloved, the end is getting close. 2 Timothy 4:5 says "But watch thou in all things, endure afflictions, do the work of an evangelist, make full prove of thy ministry". I close with James 5:11, "Behold we count them happy which endure".

TOLERANCE

Because my mother-tongue was Dutch, I learned the word tolerance at first from and in connection with mechanical engineering. I found out that tolerance is an important "law" in mechanics. It has to do with precision engineering, too little or too much of it would make the product either inoperable or break it down speedily.

For instance, a most important item in our modern mechanical world is the roller bearing. Almost everything that moves or turns uses them. If the bearing has too much tolerance in between the rollers and moving parts, it will soon disintegrate. Too little clearance or tolerance however, will give the same result or even make the moving parts entirely inoperable. In both cases, the breakdown is caused by excessive heat, which develops because of friction between the moving parts.

When I learned the biblical concept of tolerance, I discovered a great similarity between the two kinds of tolerance. The biblical concept of tolerance, of course, concerns human relationship, but here also, too much or too little of it will quickly result in a total breakdown of such relationship. The developing friction resulting in excessive heat can be compared with flaring anger which develops speedily in relationships which leads to its destruction. Of course, this is not good for a Christian brotherhood moving up to Zion in unison.

Therefore, we should aim for a brotherhood with enough tolerance between the Brethren, but not too much to be not biblical. Then the oil which symbolizes Christ-like love of the Holy Spirit, can and will lubricate the moving parts so that no excessive heat develops.

One of the most outspoken chapters in the Bible on tolerance is Romans 14. Here, God speaks about "disputable" matters (Romans 14:1). So apparently, there are matters which are neither right nor wrong in God's sight, things of which the Word does not give us a clear right or wrong. We are advised not to argue about these things. Remarkable is that in this chapter, Apostle Paul lists a number of such disputable topics as eating, drinking and even the keeping of certain days such as the Sabbath. However, even today, such things are causing much friction and division between Christians. There are vegetarians and meat eaters, alcohol users and abstainers, Sabbath keepers for Saturday or Sunday, and so on. The divisions between these Christians because of the "disputable" things are clear examples of insufficient tolerance.

On the other hand, there are also clear indications of too much tolerance, causing disobedience to God's Word and much damage to the body of Christ. To mention one example: The so-called Pluralistic concept adapted by the Methodist Church to appease the liberals. It has led to the idea that God is not the only way to salvation. This has caused great anger and division and led to a breakdown and great decline in membership.

We must realize that tolerance does not mean condoning of sin. There are many outright sins listed in God's Word and that church which condones any of them will surely fall apart. Intolerance, on the other hand, has often resulted with the sin of "exclusiveness" and the attitude of "we and only our group is right". Jesus dealt with that in Mark 9:39 and Luke 9:50, when He told the disciples not to stop other people not of their group to minister in His name. Apostle Paul shows great tolerance by saying in Philippians 1:19 "as long as Christ was preached, even out of wrong motives, he would rejoice."

Finally, it all comes down to this: "Let us love one another even as Christ has loved us". If we do that, then there will be neither too much nor too little tolerance in our relationships.

TRUST AND OBEY

Searching for a Bible verse which mentions both words, I found it only in one verse, Isaiah 50:10, although there are numerous verses talking about trusting or obeying separately. Some are implying both concepts (1 Timothy 4:19). Isaiah 50:10 is a very informative verse with a hidden promise "Who is that among you that feared the Lord, that obeyed the voice of His servant, that walketh in darkness and has no light? Let him trust in the name of the Lord and stay upon his God." This form of the Lord's question is actually implying that if you do trust and obey Him, you will never walk in darkness and remain with Him, having light all the time. Many other verses confirm this promise. Exodus 19:5 is telling us that if we obey the Lord, we will be His peculiar people! The word peculiar seems to have a negative meaning nowadays. Webster says it means "strange, queer or odd." However, in the biblical King James language, it means to be different and set aside from worldly people and called "saints" (See also 1 Peter 2:9). We sing this verse all the time! I would encourage you to look up all the verses which are telling us the benefits of trusting and obeying.

During my ministry in the Philippines, the Lord instructed me to put great emphasis on the laconic word "panactulnoc" (obedience) and I quoted John 14:15 almost every time I preached "If you love me you obey my commandments". Jesus promised us in John 15:10 that when we obey His commandment, we will abide in His love. This is one of the best comforting promises to me. In some of my former articles, I already explained that the concept of trust is rooted in faith. If you believe in the Lord Jesus Christ as your Savior, you also trust in Him. Even in our common daily language, we sometimes say "I have faith in so and so", meaning that we trust him or her. Trust is the greatest proof of honor you can give to your Lord. This is why Jesus said that unless we become like little children, we cannot enter the Kingdom of God. This is a strong warning that we must have trust in Him.

Do we really obey and trust the Lord while we are saying that we love Him? The love chapter of 1 Corinthians 13 (NIV) tells us in verse 7 that love always trusts! I do not think that an explanation of the concept of obedience is needful. Most people know what it means. James 1:22 states that we should be doers of the Word and not hearers only, and so deceiving ourselves. This entails the concept of biblical obedience. However, today there seems to be many who are "deceiving themselves". I pray and hope that this article will help you not to be one of them and that you want to trust and obey our precious Lord!

SPEAKING IN TONGUES

This time I feel led to focus in on 1 Corinthians 12:10 especially the last part "to another working of miracles, to another prophecy, to another discerning of spirits, to another diverse kind of tongues, to another interpretation of tongues." What I want you to note is that the gift of tongues is the only one of the gifts that is listed as diverse. The same thing we can notice in verse 28 of the same chapter.

Let us first define the word diverse. It means "different kinds". Webster says "of various kinds". Therefore, the logical conclusion is that when the Bible uses the word "tongues", we have to determine and discern what kind or kinds of tongues God is speaking about. What kinds does the Bible show in 1 Corinthians 12, 14 and in Acts 2?

We can readily discern three biblical kinds.

1. The kind of tongues, so foreigners could hear and understand the Lord's message spoken by the 120 believers on the day of Pentecost (Acts 2:6).
2. The kind of tongues for prayer and praise (singing) (1 Corinthians14:15, 18).

3. The kind of tongues as a prophetic message, which has to be followed by an interpretation (1 Corinthians 14:13).

Now, the first kind seems still to happen but very sporadically. This is according to some testimonies I have heard from others.

The second kind is being practiced by some Charismatic groups and Pentecostal churches. However, not as much as I would like to see because I believe strongly that in the light of the Lord's wish, we all would speak with tongues, but rather that we would prophecy (1 Corinthians 14:5).

The third kind seems to happen more and more sporadically in groups and churches and there seems to be a lack of interpreters. Now, not all seem to have this kind of gift of tongues. Because 1 Corinthians 14:30 is asking us "do all speak in tongues?" The obvious answer is no because that kind of tongues seems to be given to only a few people in the Body.

However, since the second kind of tongues is for prayer and singing (praise), it is meant by God for all spirit-filled believers. God would not withhold that from you while expressing His desire for you to practice it. Let us therefore encourage the Body of Christ to desire and practice this beautiful gift from God. It will edify us (1 Corinthians 14:4)!

FAITHFUL WOMEN

The first question needing an answer is "faithful to what?" The most complete answer seems to be faithful to the Word of God, in which He tells us what His intended role for women is. The part I want to cover here is the women's role in the work of God.

There are and have been many faithful, Godly women in God's work. Praise God! The Bible is filled with stories of women who were used by God in a great way. They were and are obedient to the Lord's calling and those from the past received a prominent place in God's Word. Most of them living now will receive their reward at the coming of Jesus. To mention a few from the past, in the Old Testament are Debora, Ruth and Esther who come to my mind. In the New Testament, those connected to the birth of Jesus who are prominent are Elizabeth, Mary and Anna. In 2 Timothy, Lois and Eunice are standing out and in Romans 15, Paul has a whole list of virtuous women who were helpful to him.

To find the Lord's intention for creating women, we have to go back to the beginning. In Genesis 2:28, it tells us that God decided to make a help-meet for Adam, "because it is not good that man should be alone". Therefore, it is biblical to say that women's primary purpose was to be a help-meet to men. As a result of the fall, I believe that God ordained women to bear children and bear them in sorrow and pain. We can conclude from this that a woman's additional purpose is to bear children. God added "your desire shall be for your husband and he shall rule over you". (Genesis 3:16)

The best biblical picture of a virtuous woman can be found in Proverbs 31, which lists her role as housewife and help-meet to her husband. It is safe to say that mostly God's Word pictures the woman as wife and mother. Therefore, we have to ask ourselves, what about unmarried and childless women? One thing is for sure, we should not judge them as cursed by God. They could be in that situation because of several different reasons in which the Lord has His hand. By the Lord's great mercy, there is also a great Godly purpose to be found for the unmarried and the childless. Those roles can be varied from case to case, but still comply with the idea that she is a help-meet to mankind.

In the family setting, the Bible tells us clearly that the wife should be subject to her husband. He is the head of the house as Christ is the Head of the church. As far as a woman's role in the church is concerned, 1 Timothy 2:9-12 is an important decisive scripture. "I do not permit a woman to teach or to have authority over a man, but be in silence." This is strong, direct language that hardly can be misunderstood. However, those in opposition still manage to reason it away with man-made hermeneutics. It is becoming more and more politically incorrect to obey what it really says. The practical outworking of this ruling is that there cannot be a woman with leadership authority in the church and this is the reason one cannot find any women elders in the New Testament.

Those disobedient people, who are still ordaining women elders, are claiming Romans 16:7 as proof that Junia was an Apostle among the Apostles. However, in most all trustworthy translations, it says only that Adronicus and Junia were well regarded among the Apostles! Actually, it is not even sure that Junia was a female, but if she was, she was most likely the wife of Adronicus. One must be very desperate to claim this as reason to disobey 1 Timothy 2.

It is true however, that husband and wife teams are mentioned sometimes, with the woman ministering under the authority of her husband. That could be done today, but one has to view this case by case for being correct, because it is being misused also. Disobedience to God's Word is increasing rapidly these last days, mainly because of our modern culture and the thinking that some of God's Word does not always apply to us today. Disobedience has eroded the true faith in our churches to the point that some now are even ordaining homosexuals! Yes, a woman can and should do vital important ministry in the church, but NEVER should take a position as a leader with authority over men.

Very remarkable, that God gives the reason for His ruling in 1 Timothy 2, which he does not do that very often! However in verse 13, He explains why. He apparently found an explanation necessary, "for Adam was first formed, then Eve". Verse 14, "And Adam was not deceived but the woman being deceived was in transgression". Some people feel that God is being unfair and holding on to an old grudge. Remember, He is our sovereign God and His ways are higher than our ways! A virtuous woman who submits herself to God and her husband is truly being and going to be blessed by God. I can testify to that because of my own faithful wife for fifty four years.

Women Elders

God's Word shows a high regard for women and that is why I was very provoked lately when some speaker suggested that enforcing God's direction in 1 Timothy 2:9-12 shows a lack of love for women. First of all, we must know that God loves all His children who have faith in Jesus Christ. He states in Galatians 3:28 "There is neither male nor female for ye are all one in Christ Jesus". Therefore, to suggest that obeying this direction in 1 Timothy 2 concerning women's roll in the church shows a lack of love is very wrong indeed.

The speaker's objection was mainly directed against the text in 1 Timothy 2:12. Let us take a good look at this instruction from the Lord. Verse 11 says: "Let the women learn in silence with all subjections". Verse 12: But I suffer not a woman to teach, nor usurp authority over the man". Other Bible versions are using the words quietness and submission. There is no way we can take this to mean something else than to say that a women should not have authority over a man, either by teaching or any other way. She should listen to them in quietness and submission and learn.

Very remarkably, this is one of the few places in God's Word where He explains why He made this ruling on women.

In the last three verses of 1 Timothy 2, He explains why He made this ruling. "For Adam was first formed then Eve and Adam was not deceived, but the women being deceived was in transgression. Not withstanding she shall be saved in childbearing, if they continue in faith and charity and holiness with sobriety." Many people do not understand or like this saying. They feel that the Lord is holding an old grudge. I hope you, reader, are not one of them!

There, does the Lord ordain elders/pastors in the church? Should we ordain elders/pastors in the church? For sure not! It is clearly shown in the New Testament that women do not occur as elders/Pastors. The speaker of last week tried to show that the Lord does give authority over men to women by telling us of his experiences with good women pastors and referring to Ruth and Esther in the Old Testament. However, although the Lord honored these faithful, Godly women, no authority over men is mentioned. Sometime ago, another person tried to prove that there was a woman Apostle in the New Testament by the name of Junia (Romans 16:7), but this is what my Bible says, "they were of note among the apostles". Several commentaries are saying that they were well regarded among the apostles.

Husband and wife teams are mentions in the New Testament and it is clear that the wives were also ministering under their husband's authority, but no position of leadership is indicated at any time. Paul is often unjustly accused of lacking respect for women, but that is opposite from what the Bible shows us. For instance, he expresses his gratitude to at least eight women in Romans 16. In Philippians 4:3, he intercedes for women who labored with him in the Gospel, while 1 Timothy 5:10 mentions Persi, "who labored much in the Lord".

There is no doubt that the Lord has used and still is using many women very mightily. They can do many things: prophecy, witness, worship and praise, comfort and help people teach other women and children. But they should not be in a position to have authority over men in the Church. It is also abundantly clear that in the family concept, the Lord has appointed the man as the head of the household, this under submission to Christ Jesus (Ephesians 5:22-24).

Today, it is also widely taught that they should be equal in authority. Submission of the woman to the husband is no more politically correct. We live in a enlightened age where the woman is liberated from oppression and that is what is being taught. But actually, they are doing great spiritual harm to a woman to allow her or appointing her to authority over a man.

I thank and praise God for the courage of the leadership of the Southern Baptist convention, who declared publicly that a woman cannot be a pastor in their churches. Please let us all obey the total Word of God. Then both men and women will be blessed by the Lord.

JUDGE NOT?

Most Christians are very much aware of this biblical admonition. However, there is a great lack of understanding of this issue. This is the reason why many Christians always object to hearing rebuke.

The main verses of "judge not" are found in Matthew 7:1-2 and Romans 2:1. What many Christians do not realize is that our Lord is talking about the wrong kind of judgment, the self-righteous, hasty, unmerciful and condemning and without cause, kind.

Most of the time when judgment is done in the Body of Christ, the people are objecting with "the judge" not the "scripture", not realizing that maybe God is wanting to expose something and is using a person in the Body to do just that!

Jesus' words in Matthew 7:1-2 are followed by verse 3, which is talking about the beam in your own eye, thus hypocritical judgment. Verse 5 mentions to remove your beam first and then the mote from your brother's eye. Jesus is requiring judgment for doing that! You have to have judgment to obey the requirement of verse 5.

The same is the case with Romans 2:1. Paul is talking about sinful, immoral and gay people, who are passing judgment while doing wrong themselves (verse 3). 1 Corinthians 4:5 speaks about judging "before time" and James 4:11-12 is talking about speaking evil or slander.

It is clear that bad judgment is condemned by God but it is also obvious from God's Word that He commands us to judge in a proper way. Many scriptures indicate the great need for us to exercise the right kind of judgment!

In Matthew 7:6, Jesus is telling us not to cast our pearls before dogs and swine's. This demands our correct judgment! In 1 Corinthians 5:3-12, Apostle Paul passes judgment on a sinner in church, not on outsiders. Some more scriptures about passing judgment are 1 Corinthians 2:15, 11:13, 14:29; Acts 17:1; 1 Thessalonians 5:21. Even our common sense, guided by the Holy Spirit will tell us that we need to pass judgment in our lives all the time and making decisions with discernment takes good judgment.

Our Lord requires us to discern right from wrong and pass judgment on all things. Many times He uses a person in the Body of Christ to pass judgment in order to bring correction ad repentance (2 Corinthians 7:9). Satan, however, is always hard at work to keep sin uncovered and out of the light. He uses people, therefore, to object to exposure.

Not many people in the Body seem to like and accept rebuke and exposure, even of others. The objection "judge not" is often heard. Special mentioning of names seemed to be condemned most of the time, but the Bible shows that our Lord wants people with names to sometimes be exposed. In 1 Timothy 1:20, for instance, Paul mentions Hymenaeus and Alexander. Notice that God's purpose is always to bring people to repentance. That He can and will be using some of you in this manner is my prayer.

WWW.COME

As computer operators, you are most likely familiar with this indicator to get to a message or program. I was wondering if the Lord could have a message like that and after giving it some thought, I came up with this lesson. The www.come stands for: work, watch and wait. The dot is the ending with His coming.

1. The first "W" for "work" is the Lord's admonition that He requires us to work. Ephesians 2:10 tells us that He created us "in Christ unto good works". In verse 8 and 9 however, He is telling us that we are saved by faith and not by our works. The disciples asked Jesus, "What shall we do to do the work of God?" and Jesus' answer was that believing in Him is the work of God. Because several times Jesus used the word "work" in connection with the harvest of souls, we can deduct that God wants us to work to win souls! To be a witness for Him everywhere was His primary concern when He went up to heaven (Acts 1:8). Another important verse to remember is James 2:20 "Faith without work is dead".

2. The second "W" stands for "watch". The New Testament is using this admonition many times. Jesus told us to watch out for false prophets and teachers, especially in the

last days. Deception is prophesied to be rampant during that time and we are now living in that time! Also, we are supposed to watch for the return of Jesus (Matthew 25:13). It is clear that God wants us to be expecting His return anytime. Luke 21:36 is also telling us to watch and pray to be worthy to escape the tribulation mentioned before. I believe that He wants us able to go up in the rapture before the wrath of God is poured out. We should be divine escape artists.

3. The third "W" is for "waiting". There are two ways in which the word "wait" is used. Waiting for and waiting on. Waiting on is usually expressed in the King James Bible as "waiting upon". We sing Isaiah 40:31 all the time, "They that wait upon the Lord shall renew their strength". "Waiting for" is mentioned in the New Testament as waiting for the return of Jesus Christ. 2 Timothy 2:13 speaks of that as "our blessed Hope". 2 Peter 3:9 says that the Lord is waiting and "longsuffering", so that we should not perish. The dot leads us to the last chapter of the Bible, Revelation 22:20 "even so, Come Lord Jesus".

Dear Friends, maybe that every time you see the www. com on your computer, you will think about the Lord's command: Work, Watch and Wait.

WHO DO YOU CALL STUPID?

Before I was baptized with the Holy Spirit in 1970, I was reading the story of the Plagues in Egypt and the demise of Pharaoh (Exodus 7-14). I thought that Pharaoh was very stupid. After all, even though he had experienced miracles and having seen the power of the Lord with the Israelites, he still wanted to pursue them through the Red Sea. Did he never get the Lord's message to let them go?

Now, however, I am reminded how stupid I have been myself, not perceiving a clear message from the Lord about my over-eating. This is what happened:

Clazina, my departed wife, who always took excellent care of me, made me daily a good lunch in a brown paper bag, which I took to work every morning. I would eat it around noon, but then walk to the closest fried chicken place to get a two-piece snack. Of course, I did not tell Clazina about this because I knew she would disapprove strongly.

So this went on for quite some time and I slowly grew fatter. One day, the chicken place had a good low priced special on a four-piece meal and I could not resist (unbiblical according to 1 Corinthians 10:13). I took the box with the chicken down to a nearby park and sat down at a bench with a table.

Amazingly, as soon as I placed the box with the chicken on the table, a strong small tornado (whirlwind) lifted my box up in the air and it went over the treetops! Then it fell down about fifty meters away on the paved road. I went to pick up the broken box and cleaned up the spilled-out pieces of chicken and still ate them!

Obviously, I did not get the Lord's message that I should not be eating so much. This to my shame and own hurt, because I became grossly over-weight and now suffer from high blood pressure and diabetes.

The Lord has forgiven me, because I did repent and in His mercy, He still let me become eighty years old. I have learned my lesson, not to be too hasty to think someone else is stupid. We might be prone ourselves to make the same mistakes. From the elderly, bridge-playing people, I have learned to say, however; "We elderly do not make stupid mistakes any longer. We only have some senior moments!"

QUESTIONING GOD

Already, this title gives the believer the sense that even this concept of questioning God is not proper. But I must confess that I myself have been doing that during several happenings in my life. I did not always have the feeling that the Lord did not like it although sometimes I was rebuked for questioning Him. To go further than this, I believe that sometimes the Lord wants to ask "why", because He has given us a message through certain occurrences in our lives and He wants us to learn something from it. To find out what the Bible is saying about our questioning Him, I have searched the Scriptures and found that there are actually two kinds of our human "whys".

The first kind, which God sometimes answers, comes from an earnest desire from us to know why certain things are happening in order to learn from it and improve into the likeness of Jesus. There are not many examples of this kind of "why" in the Bible, but there are some very significant ones. In Genesis 25:22, Rebecca, who is pregnant with Esau and Jacob, is questioning the Lord, "Why I am thus?" In verse 23, He gives her an answer, telling her in fact that the elder (Esau) will serve the younger (Jacob).

Amazingly, the Lord finds it so important for us to realize His total sovereignty that He uses this to mention this again in Romans 9:14-24. "Jacob I have loved but Esau I have hated". The Lord explains His displeasure about the clay asking the potter "Why hast Thou made me thus?"

Another good example of an apparent righteous "why" question is from Moses in Exodus 32:11. He is asking God why He is so very angry and continues to plead for His mercy. This is followed by God's mysterious statement in the King James Version, Exodus 32:14, "The Lord repented from the evil He thought to do unto His people!"

The best righteous "why" question is in the New Testament by Jesus, himself, who said "Eli, Eli, lama sabachtani "My God, My God, why hast Thou forsaken me (Matthew 27:46 and Mark 15:35)?" Father God's answer is found in most of the New Testament and especially in John 3:16. His great love for us is the reason!

The second type of our "why" is really a sign of our rebellion and disagreement with what God did or is doing. We really dislike what is happening and do not understand that our God will work His good for all of us who believe in His Son. We usually think that we know what is best, but God tells us that His thoughts are much higher and different from ours. In Romans 8:24, He states "all things work for the good to those who love God and are called according to His purpose."

I believe that most of us have been guilty of this wrong attitude in asking "why". I must confess that I have been guilty of this several times in the past when painful and unpleasant things were happening, the last time being in 2004, when Clazina, my precious wife of 55 years, died from cancer. For several weeks, I could not see the good of that and complained to the Lord asking "why". But He has mercy and has given me peace with it and forgiveness for my rebellion.

Several years ago when I was retired, we attended a Full Gospel Church. One day the main sanctuary burned down. To my dismay, the leadership and most of the members seemed to avoid the question why this had happened. Most of them seemed to say that it was just providence and something that happens normally, while others blamed the devil for it! They refused to consider that the Lord might have a message of displeasure with them and they did not learn their lesson. A good example of the Lord's displeasure with a wrong kind of why question is found in Numbers 11:20, when the Israelites were complaining about the lack of meat and asking "Why came we forth out of Egypt?" The result was the Plague with the wrath of the Lord came while the meat was still in between their teeth! I surely hope that this writing will help you to avoid the question "Why Lord?" with a wrong, disapproving attitude. We must also accept that sometimes the Lord remains quiet upon our questions. It is His prerogative.

REQUESTING GOD

Two of the best scripture verses about requesting God are Ephesians 6:18 and Philippians 4:6. Ephesians tells us several things. First of all, to pray always and Thessalonians 5:17 says "without ceasing". I conclude from this that our Lord is talking about a lifestyle of prayer and being in constant communion with Him, regardless of what we are doing.

Next supplication is mentioned. That requires our humbleness, a bowed down attitude, showing honor and respect for our Lord. Perseverance is then required and to do this for all the Saints. The Lord calls every believer in Christ a Saint because we are forgiven and washed clean from our sins by the blood of Jesus.

Philippians 4:6 is telling us not to worry about anything, but to pray for everything with supplication and thanksgiving, in order to make "our request known before God". Notice that the supplication (humbleness) is mentioned in both verses as a requirement. This means for sure that we are in agreement with God and that He has the right to answer anyway He wants! Even with a NO! When we make a "request known to God", He can say yes and fulfill our desire or He can say not now, maybe later. Also, He can and will say NO many times.

We ought to be thankful for that because we do not know what is best. We could be asking for something harmful, something that does not enhance the Kingdom of our Lord and even could be harmful to our soul.

This required humble attitude is a far cry from some of the popular ways people are claiming today. It has been taught, that in order to show our great faith, we can claim in our prayers and remind God of some promises!

A claim means that something already belongs to you and that God cannot say no. This is in direct conflict with humble asking with supplication and our Lord will not listen to such prayer. Please never claim anything with the Lord. Always ask with supplication and thanksgiving!

That the Lord turns a deaf ear to some prayers is a biblical fact and it is something different than Him just saying no. When the Lord refuses to hear a prayer, it goes not even up to heaven. The psalmist says that if you regard iniquity in your heart, heaven will be like brass (Psalm 66:18)! There are several scriptures like that. In Isaiah 59:1-2, God hides His face because of sin. "When you do not hear the cry of the poor you shall not be heard" (Proverbs 21:13). Zechariah 7:10-13 is virtually saying the same thing, but adding the crying of widows, orphans and strangers.

The New Testament also lists conditions from our Lord for hearing and answering our prayers. Humbleness with supplication, thanksgiving, and praying according to His will in the name of Jesus are some of the very obvious ones. 1 John 3:22 is telling us to obey His commands and do things that are pleasing in the Lord's sight, in order "to receive of Him".

Some hindrances to answered prayers are unforgiveness and pride. 1 Peter 3:7 lists mistreatment of wives also as a hindrance to prayer. I certainly hope that this short article will help you to have effective prayers which are pleasing to the Lord.

CONCLUSION-OPINION-ASSUMPTION-PRESUMPTION

These four "ion's" are usually following each other in our thinking and these sometimes end up in presumption. Psalm 19:13 shows us that our Lord really does not like "presumptuous sins". King David's prayer, "Keep back thy servant also from presumptuous sins; let them not have dominion over me; then I shall be upright and I shall be innocent from the great transgression". I believe that the great transgression is the disobedience to our Lord's directions. Notice also that it says sins (multiple), thus, there are several sins of this kind.

Deuteronomy 7:9-13 is talking about inquiring from the Lord and verse 12 even requires death if the directions are not followed! Verse 13 orders people to hear and fear and not to act presumptuously. 2 Peter 2:10 is mentioning presumption as part of unjust self-willed people, so there is no doubt that God dislikes presumption on our part very much. James 4 is talking about presuming about tomorrow.

We all seem to be very prone to presumption. When the Lord warned me against this, I started thinking about the background and cause of this sin. I came to the conclusion that it is usually based on wrong conclusions and assumptions. For teachers, it results in influencing others the wrong way and causing harm to the Body of Christ. During my life, I have experienced several Christian teachers who were well meaning and Godly but committing this mistake in their teachings. I want to tell about three examples like that.

1. In some seminars, I heard teaching that Jesus apparently did something deliberately, as an example: Jesus healing deliberately on the Sabbath in order to provoke the Pharisees. Scripture does not tell us that and it is based on human thinking and a faulty conclusion.

2. When people, who believe the doctrine of "once saved, always saved", are reading about our strong security in Christ and our eternal security, they apparently go a step farther and conclude that one can not loose his eternal life once you are saved. Again, this is a wrong conclusion.

3. From the start, when I was baptized with the Holy Spirit in 1970, I have spoken in tongues and maybe I can say that I speak in tongues as much as any Pentecostal person. I value it very much. However, I do not agree with the doctrine that it is the "evidence" of having been baptized with the Holy Spirit. This doctrine is mainly based on the assumption that, because the believers in Cornelius house in Acts 10 assumed that the tongue speakers had received the Holy Spirit as they had; therefore it is "the evidence".

Can we really make this assumption on this basis? I believe not, because the word "evidence" is from the English law system which recognizes true and false evidence. In the case of tongue-speakers, there are evidently many who have the false kind of evidence! Even some Mormons are speaking in tongues! Again, a wrong assumption/

conclusion followed by a wrong opinion, which is doing a great harm to the Body of Christ.

This evidence doctrine turns off those people in the Body who for some reason are not yet speaking in tongues. It causes a great split instead of promoting brotherly love and oneness. From God's Word, we can tell that we should look for a powerful ability to lead a Godly life and be an effective witness for Christ. So please, do not adapt this "evidence" theory, which brings disunity in the church.

THE PROVIDENCE OF GOD

"It just happened!" Many people seem to say that when observing some bad happenings. This sounds fatalistic to me and not according to God's Word.

I was stirred up to think about the Providence of our God when I read a morning devotion, in which the writer stated that trouble is not only inevitable, but also indiscriminate. Perhaps the writer was thinking about the saying of Jesus in Matthew 5:45, "God makes the sun to rise and the rain to fall on the evil and on the good, and sends rain on the just and the unjust". It was particularly the word "indiscriminate" that made me think, because if we acknowledge God's Providence in everything, can we then accuse Him of indiscrimination? I believe and the Bible indicates that our God is involved in everything that is happening and that He is accomplishing His purpose always. The word "indiscrimination", according to Webster, means "haphazard and at random". Maybe our writer did not mean that?

From experience, I come to the conclusion that even many Christians do not accept the total Providence of our God which is to their great harm, because fatalism brings much depression. I found a very good article on the subject of the Providence of God on the internet. I want to share it with you and maybe you want to look it up for yourself. It is under www.geocities. It lists many scriptures of which I will mention some and ask you to look up the texts yourself. The Bible indeed shows overwhelming evidence that our God is totally involved in everything.

Mentioning now some scriptures about God's involvement with a purpose:

1. God's purpose is unstoppable (Isaiah 46:9-10)!
2. God causes men to do His will (Ezra 1:1, Proverbs 21:30, Daniel 1:9, Exodus 4:4, Genesis 39:21).
3. God controls all details of our lives (Job 14:50), length of our days (John 3:27), makes us rich or poor (Isaiah 2:7), gives children (Psalm 127:3), or withholds them (1 Samuel 1:5), God enables to conceive (Ruth 4:13), sets boundaries where they may live (Acts 17:26), gives wisdom (Daniel 2:21).
4. Sets the rulers over us (Daniel 4:17) and gives kingdoms to whom He wishes (Daniel 4:25).
5. God controls all weather, wind, lightening, snow, and rain (Psalm 135:7, Job 37:6-13).
6. Feeds and cares for animals (Matthew 6:26, 10:29).
7. Finally, He gives the purpose for raising you up. (Romans 9:17).

There is absolutely no indication that God limits His control over humans (Daniel 4:35). The Bible declares that humans are not in control (Jeremiah 10:23, Proverbs 16:9).

To sum it all up, God works out everything (Ephesians 1:11)! In Lamentations 3:37, God is asking "Who can speak and make it happen?" Then in Lamentations 3:38, He says "Is it not from the mouth of the Most High that both evil and good things come?" Now, the King James Version uses the word "evil" for both sin and calamities. Sin does not come from the Lord; therefore, He is talking here about calamities.

In Isaiah 45, the Lord uses the word "I" many times, indicating that He wants us to know that He is sovereign and doing everything according to His good pleasure. In verse 7, He tells us that He created light as well as darkness, well-being as well as calamities! Also in Amos 3:6, "Shall there be evil (calamity) in a city and the Lord has not done it?" For sure, the Lord is involved in both good and bad!

For instance, take the suffering Jesus. It was God's plan (Acts 2:23, Isaiah 53:10). He is even involved in our decisions and uses the bad for our good (Genesis 50:20). So does belief in God's total providence and sovereignty make us fatalistic? Absolutely not, but the opposite is true. Fatalism is negative and causes depression, but we can and should rejoice in God's total involvement in our lives and in the world. The knowledge that God is even in our troubles can comfort and help us.

COERCION

Thinking about the controversial subject of men's free will, the word "coercion" came to me. When I learned English, I perceived that the general connotation is very negative. Looking now in the Webster dictionary, I found that this is not necessarily always true because Webster states as explanation number one "to restrain or dominate by nullifying individual will." However, the second and third explanations are mentioning the use of force and threat. No wonder that English-speaking people do not like to be coerced this way and the connotation is as something undesirable and bad.

If we take Webster's first definition of restraining and dominating, could we not use this concept in relation to the acts of God in our lives? Do we not need to be restrained and dominated by our God?

As for me, I certainly have the need in my life for God's restrained and domination in my life! I believe that it is very biblical. Our sovereign God can and does use any method of His choice to bring us to repentance!

Where does this leave us as far as our so-called "free will"? Some time ago, I wrote an article and made the statement that maybe men's free will is a misnomer. I pointed out that even in our decision-making, our Lord is involved. The surprising statement of Jesus in John 15:16, that He has chosen us and we did not choose Him, made me look into the doctrine of our free choice.

I found out from Bible research that God indeed wants us to make choices. Joshua 24:15 is the clearest verse. It says "Choose you this day whom you will serve". Praise His Holy Name! God also let David choose which of the three options for punishment he would prefer.

However, John 15:16 and other Bible verses, indicate that the Lord is directly involved when we have to make choices, even to the point so that we choose what He wants us to choose!

I really wonder how it is possible that we still remain responsible for our own choice. However, this is absolutely also a biblical fact! It seems that Our Lord is unfair; however, I know that this is not true because our God is always just and fair. The Bible indicates this and we must accept and believe God's Word.

From Bible stories like the one in 2 Chronicles 22:23, where it states that the Lord sent a lying spirit, we can deduct that the Lord does coerce. Also, other stories like the refusals of Pharaoh in Exodus 9 is telling us that God hardened Pharaoh's heart many time and Pharaoh was still sinning! There is no doubt however, that we remain responsible for our choices.

We must understand that our God is all-knowing and maybe He coerces people who are already bent on sinning and have an evil heart. Considering all this, we can understand that we only have a limited free will and that the Lord is involved in everything we choose. The Lord is conducting us continuously. We can trust Him that all things work for the good to them that love God and are called according to His purpose (Romans 8:28).

I am glad that our Lord restrains and dominates me, but I pray that I will grow more in the likeness of Jesus so that I will always obey Him out of my love for Him. How about you?

THE PRECIOUS GIFT OF TONGUES

In 1 Corinthians 12, our Lord lists nine Gifts of the Spirit. In verse 1, He starts out by saying that "He does not want us to be ignorant about the Spiritual Gifts". Yet, among the Bible-believing Christians, there is a great amount of ignorance and misunderstanding about the gifts, especially the gift of tongues. Although this teaching will focus on tongues, for completeness sake and the context, I am listing the nine gifts here: word of wisdom; word of knowledge; faith; working of miracles; gifts of healing; prophecy; discerning of spirits; divers or different kinds of tongues; interpretation of tongues.

It is a sad fact that this precious gift of tongues is so controversial and seems to create a lot of strife. Therefore, let us take a close look at what God's Word reveals about this. If we truly love God, His desire should be our command. His desire is that we are not ignorant about this! In obedience, meditate over this teaching and then bring it into practice.

The Different Viewpoints

To start out with, we should mention that a sincere and rather large group of Christians are "against" speaking in tongues. Some want to forbid its practice in the church altogether. Their reasons, which I have heard, are: "It is too emotional and Pentecostal." "It causes strife in the body." "Apostle Paul rebukes the Corinthian church for it." "It was only for then in the beginning." It creates two classes of Christians, one claiming to be more spiritual than the other."

Of course, there are many churches who seem to ignore the subject altogether.

In the face of the clear teaching in God's Word, you wonder why this is. I believe I know the answer. Satan understands the tremendous benefits for the believer who exercises this gift. Therefore, he does his utmost to bring it in disrepute! When believers reject the Lord's gift, it is like a slap in the Lord's face! He also counterfeits this gift often times with great success. Imagine your father or best friend offering you a gift and you rejecting it!

There are several scriptures these believers need to absorb. Quoting from 1 Corinthians 14:1, "Pursue love and desire spiritual gifts, but especially that you may prophecy". Verse 4: "He who speaks in tongues edifies himself", etc. Verse 5: "I wish you all spoke with tongues", etc. Verse 14: "For if I pray in a tongue my spirit prays", etc. Verse 18: "I thank my God; I speak with tongues more than you all". Verse 37-38: "If any man think himself to be a prophet, or spiritual, let him acknowledge that the things that I write unto you are the commandments of the Lord." If these Christians love the Lord, I really do not need to add any further rebuke.

Then there are many Christians who say that they are not against this gift of tongues, but they believe it is not for them and therefore, the Lord does not give it to them. However, many times you can detect an antipathy towards this gift in their Spirit. The defense they have and quickly bring out is 1 Corinthians 12:30 which is Paul's question "do all speak in tongues?" Obviously this has to be answered with "No, not all Christians do". To draw the conclusion out of this that the Lord is telling us that this gift is not for all is very wrong. If this was true, then the Lord is contradicting Himself in 1 Corinthians 14:5. "I wish you all speak in tongues". He was simply just pointing out that not all do. I believe He was talking about the special kind of tongues which is equal to prophecy and has to be followed by interpretation. This is clear from the context with the rest of the question, "Do all interpret?"

However, the non-tongue-speaker will usually quickly refer to 1 Corinthians 12:25 as context that it brings schism in the body! All the while they do not realize that as an excuse for their unwillingness, they accuse the Lord of having a bad gift or having refused it to them!

For those who earnestly desire spiritual gifts, including tongues, this teaching is for the purpose to help them to receive this precious gift. The situation is not helped much by those who do exercise it themselves, but tell the have-nots that it is alright not to have it. Many tongue-speakers seem to have the need to be tolerant with this and therefore teach that it is alright with the Lord not to desire the gift of tongues! Most of the time, this is caused by a misunderstanding of 1 Corinthians 12:30, "do all speak with tongues?"

Another reason is that many do not discern that there are "diverse or different types of tongues" and that Paul referred in his question to the specific kind of tongues which has to be followed by interpretation. The result is that today we have many so-called spiritual worship leaders who are not able to use tongues, this, while scripture tells us to sing and pray in tongues (1 Corinthians 14:15). Therefore, we can say, the blind are trying to lead the blind! 1 Corinthians 14:5 does day this "I wish you all spoke with tongues, but even more that you prophesied, for he who prophesies is greater than he who speaks with tongues, unless he indeed interprets, that the church may receive edification". The addition to "I wish you all spoke with tongues" in not way, takes away from the fact that it is the will of God that we all speak with tongues! It only makes clear that tongues are on par with prophecy when followed by interpretation!

The Diverse or Different Types of Tongues

It is essential that we understand that the gift of tongues is "diverse or of different kinds". It is the only gift listed like that. Notice though, that when Paul speaks about the gifts, the word "diversity" is used several times in 1 Corinthians 12. In a way, you could say that the gift of tongues consists out of several gifts connected to "strange tongues" (not your own language). If you do not discern this, you will have a problem to understand "Do all speak in tongues?" and "He who speaks in a tongue does not speak to me but to God" or "I thank God I speak with tongues more than you all, yet in church I would rather speak five words with my understanding".

These scriptures have to be seen in the light that there are at least three different types of tongue gifts. Studying God's Word, we can readily observe three different kinds.

1. In Acts 2, on the day of Pentecost, the gift of tongues is used to clear the barrier of foreign languages, to let the foreigners understand them. It could be still in operation

today. I have heard some testimonies to that end but also heard stories about missionaries who refused to learn foreign languages and fell flat on their faces. They were too zealous for this particular kind of tongue and presumptuous and therefore failed.

2. The gift of tongues being exercised as a prophetic message to the believer, which must be followed by the gift of interpretation (1 Corinthians 14:13; 14:5). Then it is on par and equal to the gift of prophecy (verse 5).

3. When Paul states in verse 18 his thanks to God for his gift of tongues, he is referring to the kind he is using in his praise and worship. We must conclude that, because he adds "I rather speak with understanding in church". There are also several exhortations to pray, sing and worship in tongues, which are called speaking to God, not to men.

So, here we have already three different kinds of tongues. Distinctly different from each other that you could say they are three different gifts. We must consider that in order to clearly understand what He is trying to tell us. When Paul states the question "do all speak in tongues", he is definitely talking about the tongues being used as prophecy. Not all are used by the Lord that way. The statement "I wish you all spoke in tongues" pertains clearly to the tongues used for prayer, worship and praise. Keep in mind the Lord never contradicts Himself!

The Use in Prayer, Praise and Worship

The tongues, which are for every believer, are the one used for prayer, praise and worship because that is what the Lord desires from every believer. We must worship Him in spirit and truth. God found it necessary to record Paul's statement in 1 Corinthians 14:37, "The things I write are the commands of God". He apparently foresaw that some people would not be able to accept what Paul is saying. In 1 Corinthians 14:15, Paul's admonition to us is "I will pray with the Spirit, and I will also pray with the understanding. I will sing with the Spirit and also with the understanding." This conclusion he gives after he explains the difference between the prophetic tongues and the private worship tongues. This admonition to use tongues for worship and prayer is also given in several other scriptures. Colossians 3:16 – to worship with psalms hymns, and spiritual songs. Ephesians 5:19 – to be filled with the Spirit, also then using tongues in spiritual songs. Jude 21 is speaking about building ourselves up in our most holy faith, praying in the Holy Spirit.

Although these three scriptures do not specifically mention tongues, it is implied.

For All Believers

Does the Lord want the gift of tongues for all believers? The answer is a qualified YES! It is qualified because there is definite proof in God's Word for it. Let us consider the following:

A. Acts 2:1. When the day of Pentecost had fully come, they were ALL with one accord in one place. These all consisted of about 120 followers of Jesus as mentioned in Acts 1:15. Now, think about this! Anytime when you have 120 believers together, there are all kinds of people among them. From babes in Christ to well matured followers. Assuredly, there were some still struggling with old sins and bad habits. This is likely since Jesus ministered only for three years and many could have been very recent converts. Yet amazingly, the Lord chooses to baptize them ALL with the Holy Spirit and give them ALL the gift of tongues! He did not determine that some of the 120 were not worthy to receive that gift. This idea should be of tremendous encouragement to those who are seeking for this gift. It was to me a vital discovery that it is not a matter of worthiness.

When I was seeking some thirty years ago, I was still smoking. I thought that it kept me from receiving, but the Lord sent me a man who told me that his father was actually smoking when he got baptized with the Holy Spirit. It opened my eyes to the Lord's attitude. Shortly after I received the baptism with the Holy Spirit and gift of tongues, the Lord helped me to stop smoking. If you wait until you are worthy enough, you might never receive! Are you one of those who do desire but are not receiving because deep in your heart you feel unworthy? "Come unto Me and drink" cried Jesus in John 7:37!

B. The fact that He gave all 120 believers the gift of tongues is right in line with His Word. 1 Corinthians 14:5 states "I wish you ALL spoke with tongues, etc." Although prophecy is greater unless you follow with interpretation, it does not diminish the fact it is the Lord's wish for ALL!

Receiving the Gift

The only qualification there is for receiving the Baptism with the Holy Spirit and the gift of tongues is to be a Bible-believing, born again Christian who is thirsty. How do you receive it? By faith, just like you received your salvation with eternal life. James 1:7 states that you cannot receive anything from the Lord without faith. You have received a measure of faith, so put it to work! John 7:37 tells us that Jesus stood up and cried out: "If any man thirst, let him come unto me and drink. He that believes, as the scripture has said, out of his belly shall flow rivers of living water". We can grasp the importance of this statement by the fact that the Lord wanted to make sure that we understand what He was talking about. In the following verse 39, He gives a full explanation what He meant to say, "But this He spoke concerning the Spirit, whom those believing in him would receive; for the Holy Spirit was not yet given, because Jesus was not yet glorified."

After Jesus went to heaven and was glorified, it happened on the day of Pentecost. Remarkably, He is comparing the Baptism with the Holy Spirit with drinking living water and the tongues following with rivers of this water flowing out of us! The thirsty believer is invited to come and drink. Therefore, the question is, "Are you thirsty?" Then go to Jesus and receive. It is as simple as that!

1 Corinthians 14:4 says "He that speaketh in an unknown tongue edifies himself, but he that prophesies edifies the church". What does edifying yourself mean? It means building yourself up in faith and holiness. Do we need that? You better believe it! Edifying yourself or building yourself up is a necessary requirement for every believer. Jude 20 exhorts us to do it and at the same time links it with "praying in the Holy Ghost", that is with tongues. When Paul compares edifying the church with edifying yourself, he certainly is not putting the last down! Every one of us needs edification!

In opposition to some Pentecostal denominations that hold to the doctrine that speaking in tongues are THE EVIDENCE of the baptism with the Holy Spirit, I am convinced that you can receive the baptism and not speak in tongues. Apparently, some believers have, but it is not the Lord's desire! It is because of some blockage in the spirit of the receiver that tongues do not occur. The Lord in His great mercy still baptizes them! Now to call tongues the EVIDENCE of the baptism is going way beyond scripture. Acts 10:46 seems to be their only justification for this stand. It says that when those of the circumcision (Jews) believed that the Holy Ghost had been poured out on the Gentiles in the gathering at Cornelius' house because "they heard them speak with tongues". Now this is the only direct indication that they took that as evidence!!!

The Evidence

The word "evidence" itself is not a biblical word. It comes from the original English law system. The big drawback of using such a word is that there are two kinds of evidence: true and false evidence! Therefore, using such a word in a statement of doctrine does not render any help in evaluation! In addition, this doctrine at the same time, renounces all the believers who believe themselves that they received the baptism without tongues and therefore do not exercise tongues. Certainly, it is wrong to call it the evidence. This is what really causes schisms in the body!

Satan is capable of counterfeiting all the gifts of the Spirit and seems to concentrate especially on tongues. I believe it is so because he realizes the great importance of this gift. The result is there are many false tongue-speakers. The dis-reputation these false tongue-speakers bring causes great harm to the body of Christ.

It is Not Too Late!

For those who believe and know that they are baptized with the Holy Spirit but cannot speak with tongues, the best advice is to overcome whatever hindrance was and is. Go to Jesus with a repenting heart and receive by BEGINNING! By faith, the Spirit will then give you utterance. Scripture reveals that you have to begin. In Acts 2:4, the way it tells us about the Pentecostal experience is very significant!

It says "they were ALL filled with the Holy Ghost and BEGAN to speak with other tongues as the Spirit gave them utterance". BUT, THEY HAD TO BEGIN! As long as you do not open your mouth using your tongue by faith, the Spirit does not give you the utterance. The just shall live by faith, so why do you not begin?

Much ignorance on the baptism with the Holy Spirit has been caused by the churches neglect to teach. Many believers are asking "But did I not have the Spirit when I got saved?" Of course you had the Spirit! The Word says that you cannot even come to Jesus unless the Spirit of God draws you and from the moment you are born again, the Spirit will abide WITH YOU. But it takes an additional step of faith and obedience to receive the baptism and then the Spirit will be in you! (John 14:17) It is clear that there are at least two volumes of the Holy Spirit: enough and not enough!

In the Parable of the Ten Virgins, five of them had enough oil (Holy Spirit) to the end, but the other five did not have enough. Would you like to be wise and have enough of the Holy Spirit? Would you like to be like one of his 120 followers, obey His command, come to the Pentecostal upper room and receive the Living Waters and having it overflow out of you? I pray, may your answer be "Yes, Lord!"

The Shortage of Oil

The economy of the West seems to depend completely on a sufficient supply of oil. The oil cartels are pushing the oil price up nowadays by limiting the supplies. It is affecting our energy production and transportation to the point that it brings our standard of living down. Yes, the shortage has a very serious effect on our lives!

The Bible also mentions a shortage of oil, which has an even more serious effect on us. It affects our spiritual lives. The oil in the Bible represents, most of the time, the Holy Spirit of God. In the Parable of the Ten Virgins (Matthew 25:1-13), Jesus is giving us a serious warning about a shortage of that kind of oil. The purpose of this parable is to make sure that we have enough oil to keep our lamps shining until the end.

All ten virgins had shining lamps with oil to keep them burning, but only half of them had an extra supply of oil. The other five ran out of oil because the bridegroom's coming was delayed. The result was that they were rejected by Jesus and could not enter the wedding feast.

Therefore, the most important question is: How can we make sure that we have enough oil (power) to make it till the end? Well, Jesus gives the answer in John 7:37-

38 and Acts 1:8! In John, He indicates that we should be thirsty enough to come to Jesus and in verse 39, Father God explains that He was talking about the Baptism with the Holy Spirit, which was to come later after He had gone to heaver.

Jesus, with His last word here on earth, said "you shall receive power after the Holy Ghost has come upon you" (Acts 1:8). He was talking about the Baptism with the Holy Spirit right before that (see verse 5). Verse 8 also tells us the purpose of the Baptism with the Holy Spirit so that we can let our lamps shine, having enough oil, everywhere in the world.

We need to give special attention to the word "receive" because we have to be willing to receive it! It is not automatic or coerced, but it is offered to the believers and it has to be received. Jesus is coming back very soon and will have His wedding feast. That is why the question "do you have enough oil" is so urgent. Make sure that you belong to the five wise virgins group and get enough oil.

THE BOGEYMAN

Webster's Dictionary defines "bogeyman" as an imaginary monstrous figure to threaten children. I am using this word, because many people seem to see Satan as the bogeyman who threatens God's children. For sure, however, he is real and the Bible shows us that he wants to do us harm (1 Peter 5:8). The Bible also shows us that there is no need for God's children to have a fear for Satan. We need to know our enemy, but not fear him.

In Luke 12:4, Jesus is telling us rather to fear Him, who after He kills has the power to cast into hell and of course, He is talking about our Father God, whom we should fear. If you have fear for the devil, you should take a good look at some Bible verses.

The first one is short and somewhat hidden and therefore seems insignificant, but it is of great importance. John 14:30: "The prince of this world is coming and has nothing in me." God's secret revealed here is that when we are covered by the blood of Jesus, Satan has no ground to hinder us. This idea should give us encouragement. God's admonition is: "And have no fellowship with the unfruitful works of darkness" (Ephesians 5:11).

Someone has said that you cannot prevent the devil to fly over your head, but you certainly can prevent him to make a nest in your hair!

Then, James 4:8 is God's instruction on how to deal with the evil one. It should give us great comfort: "Draw night unto God, resist the devil and he will flee from you". It seems to me that the evil one has absolutely no chance to bother us when we obey our Lord's instruction.

When the Bible shows occasions that the devil was bothering God's children, it always indicates that God had to allow it. There is an outstanding story about that in both the Old and New Testaments. The book of Job shows clearly that the devil is in submission to our Father God. Jesus reveals in Luke 22:31 that Satan desired to sift Peter like wheat. Jesus prayed that Peter's faith would not fail and that in the end, it would strengthen the Brethren. When our Father God allows Satan to bother us, He always works it out for our good! (Romans 8:28)

Most of us confess to the absolute power of our God and we believers in Jesus Christ are God's children. Therefore, should we not assume that our powerful Heavenly Father will protect us from the evil one? There is no need to worry about attacks from bogeyman!

The Bible expresses our need to have confidence in our loving Heavenly Father several times. Romans 8:31 states: "What shall we say then to these things, if God be for us, who can be against us?" Then continuing in Verse 38-39, it is listing ten occasions to point out that nothing can separate us from the love of God. Are you persuaded of that?

For certain, it is not the bogeyman we should fear. We should focus our attention on ourselves. God and the devil are not the only spiritual forces in the universe. God has created us also with a Spirit. Watchman Nee with his book,

"The Latent Power of the Soul", has opened my eyes to the fact that originally we had spiritual power for the good, but after the disobedience of Adam and Eve, this power went latent. However, it can become active and working for the good through the Second Adam, Jesus Christ. When we get born again, all things become new and we get a new nature. Hallelujah!

If we are tempted to sin, we should not conform to this world but be transformed by the renewing of our mind: then we will prove the good and acceptable and perfect will of God (Romans 12:2). When we do fail sometimes, we can only blame ourselves. Most of our temptations are coming from our own mind. God mentions temptations as "common to man" (1 Corinthians 10:13) and He is giving us the promise that He will not suffer (allow) us to be tempted above that we are able to stand. But, He will with the temptation also, make a way of escape! This should comfort us a great deal.

So, if we fall for the temptation, it is entirely our own fault, but our loving Heavenly Father has an antidote for our guilt. Through Jesus our Lord, "If we confess our sins, He is faithful and just to forgive our sins and cleanse us from all unrighteousness" (1 John 1:9). God is so good!

THE BABY

A very common saying is "throwing the baby away with the bath water". This came to my mind when I was reading a religious magazine article about excesses of the Charismatic Renewal. For the most part, I agreed with the writer about the strange and unbiblical teachings that developed since the beginning of the Charismatic Renewal. It caused many believers to desire and experience many strange manifestations of the so-called presence of God. A prime example was the laughing revival in Toronto. However, when the writer declared that the absence of reference to the day of Pentecost after Acts 2 in the New Testament was an indication that God did not want us to experience any manifestations, I did feel that many so-called good evangelical Christians are throwing the baby away with the dirty bath water. The baby, in this case, is the Gifts of the Holy Spirit.

The result is a great lack of spiritual power in the Christian Church mission. It is a proven fact today that those people who are experiencing and practicing the Gifts of the Holy Spirit have far more result from their mission work than those who are negative about the Charismatic Renewal. This is not so strange, considering the statement of Jesus in His last words of Acts 1:8, "You shall receive power". All nine Gifts of the Holy Spirit which are listed in 1 Corinthians 12 are manifestations given by God to help us to be more spiritual and stronger Christians. It causes us to have more impact on the unbelieving world, including the much maligned gift of tongues.

To look at this another way, we all realize that prayer is absolutely necessary for our spiritual well-being, which is required for being a good witness. Well, the Bible declares that we actually do not know how to pray, but that the Holy Spirit can make intercession for us in our prayers, crying Abba Father with sounds we cannot produce. The divine gift of healings also can have a powerful effect on the unbelieving world.

We should never forget that our God wants us to eagerly desire spiritual gifts (1 Corinthians 14:1). I hope you all are just eagerly doing that!

THE LOVE AND THE HATE OF GOD

The concept that God is love is well known and accepted by most Christians. It is clearly stated in 1 John 4:8. In a discussion about God's love for us, someone said "God hates sin but loves the sinner". Somehow, Romans 6:23 came to my mind, which says "the wages of sin is death: but the gift of God is eternal life through Jesus Christ our Lord." I believe that the Holy Spirit reminded me of this so that we will not think that God condones sin and sinners.

Upon researching this matter, I found that the Bible indeed, supports that God loves sinners. "God so loved the world that He gave" states this in John 3:16. There is no reason to limit the word "world". God is talking here about all of sinful human mankind. Thus His love for sinners caused Him to give us Jesus. Another verse that supports this idea is Romans 5:8, "When we were yet sinners, Christ died for us".

Having said all this, we must be aware also of the fact that God teaches us in His Word that He hates sin and the sinner! The sin and the sinner can really not be separated. In Psalm 5:5-7, workers of iniquity are called foolish and God states that He hates them!

In Proverbs 6:16-19, our God lists seven things which He hates and all of them are done by parts of the human body: eyes, ears, tongues, hands and feet, but most of all, the human heart, which devises wicked imaginations. These seven things are not the only things God hates! There are many more in the Bible, among which is divorce (Malachi 2:16). There is therefore no doubt that He hates sin and the sinners!

It seems here that we are dealing with a direct contradiction! However, God never contradicts Himself. We, in our human weakness of understanding, are only coming to wrong conclusions! The key to understand the tension between God's love and hate are the words "conditional" and "unlimited", because both concepts of God's love and hate are to some extent conditional and limited.

For instance, John 3:16 states that "God gave". Now, something that is given has to be received or accepted, for only when we receive the gift can it become beneficial to us. The condition here is that we believe in Jesus. Verse 18 states we are condemned already if we do not believe in Jesus. Clearly from this, is that although God, in his love for sinners, gave us His only begotten Son to atone for our sin. We bring condemnation on ourselves if we refuse to believe in Jesus.

It appears to me that this is not brought out enough in our evangelism. There seems to be a tendency to talk only about God's love, this while avoiding to tell them about the consequences of their rejection. It is a form of sugar-coating the gospel when we avoid mentioning the wrath of God. Hell and brim-fire preachers of old were usually looked upon very negatively and maybe righteously so, if this was the main emphasis. However, there is a definite need to teach the fear of God and His wrath, besides preaching the love of God.

This seems to be the age of tolerance, by which everything goes. They are using the term "political correctness". Do not rock the boat! But, many times God wants us to rock the boat and tell people about God's anger and wrath in addition to His redeeming love. That is why there is much in the Bible on "the fear of the Lord."

It would be good for Christians to go for a good Bible dictionary, like Young's Analytical and look at all the verses to find out what pleases the Lord and what He hates. To end this admonition, "Know that the Lord is slow to anger and will not at all acquit the wicked". (Naham 1:3). Have confidence in God because "the earth is full of God's goodness" (Psalm 33:5).

REWARDS

There is no doubt that most people like receiving rewards and that rewards are powerful motives for many people's actions. The idea of "what can I get out of this?" did not appear to me very spiritual, especially in the context of being godly. However, after studying the Bible, I came to the conclusion that Our Lord is using rewards as an encouragement for us to become godlier.

The Bible is full of the word "reward" and uses the word in a negative sense as well; as recompense for evil. For instance, He rewards evildoers with destruction.

However, I am focusing here on the fact that our Lord is using His rewards to bring us to belief and good works. Hebrew 11:6 states that we must believe that He is and that He is a rewarder of them that *diligently seek Him*.

Both with the fear of the Lord and the rewards of the Lord, God gives us a powerful biblical motive to live Godly lives! The fear of the Lord and the rewards of the Lord as concepts together are found in Psalm 19:9-11: "The fear of the Lord is clean, enduring forever: the judgments of the Lord are true and righteous altogether. More to be desired are they than gold, yea, than fine gold: sweeter also than honey and the honeycomb. Moreover by them is thy servant warned: and in keeping of them THERE IS GREAT REWARD."

Already in Genesis 15:1, the Lord started to use the reward concept. In His promise to Abraham, He promised to be his shield and EXCEEDINGLY GREAT REWARD! But, all through the Bible, God indicates there are rewards for righteousness (Psalm 58:11); He rewards many godly actions as well as service in the tabernacle (Numbers 18:3); God rewards working with two together (Ecclesiastics 4:9); sowing in righteousness (Proverbs 11:18); abiding in work and labor (1 Corinthians 3:8,14) and willingly preaching the Gospel (1 Corinthians 9:17).

Jesus Himself, promised great rewards when you are persecuted and reviled for His sake (Matthew 5:11). He also said that we shall in no way lose our reward when we just give a cup of water in His name (Matthew 10:42). In Matthew 6, He is talking about giving alms, praying and fasting in secret, which will be openly rewarded.

I believe that our greatest reward is found in Colossians 3:24. It speaks of our reward as "our inheritance" when we heartily serve God. Our inheritance is eternal life with our God in Heaven. Jesus is coming back very soon and the Bible declares that He is bringing His rewards with Him. That was already prophesied by Isaiah at least twice (Isaiah 40:10; 62:1) and repeated in Revelation 22:12.

Are you diligently seeking our Lord? Then He will reward you by being found and getting blessed during your lifetime and forever with Him in heaven.

THEREFORE, IF

Our Lord God is using these seemingly common and ordinary words for matters of great importance to us, His people. I remember from the 1970's Bob Mumford saying, "When there is a therefore in God's Word, you better determine what the therefore is there for".

There are also many "ifs" in the Bible. Many are there to show us how our God wants us to behave. For instance, it is often followed by conditions for receiving something from Him. This is why I started looking for scriptures in which God is using these words. In two scripture, I found that the Lord is using both words together in one sentence!

Starting in the Old Testament, the Lord writes in Exodus 19:5, "Now THEREFORE IF you will obey my voice indeed and keep my covenant, then ye shall be as a peculiar treasure unto me, above all people: for all the earth is mine". The "therefore" here is the reason given in verse 4, where God reminded His people that He delivered them from Egypt and brought them unto Himself with great miracles as on eagle wings! I believe that God is speaking here to every born-again Christian. The word "if" shows here the condition for us to become a peculiar people. This condition is to be obedient to God's voice.

God uses the word "peculiar" also in the New Testament. See Titus 2:14 "and purify Himself a peculiar people" as well as 1 Peter 2:9, "but ye are a peculiar people".

The original meaning of the word "peculiar" was different from what it is today. Earlier in the use of the English language, it meant "out of the ordinary, set apart and precious". Did you know that you are a peculiar person and precious, different and set apart unto our Lord? Do you realize that obeying God's voice is the condition?

In the New Testament, the Lord reverses the THEREFORE IF. Revelation 3:3 states, "Remember therefore how that thou hast received and heard and repent. IF THEREFORE thou shall not watch, I will come on thee as a thief and thou shall not know what hour I will come upon thee." In 1 Thessalonians 5:4, the Lord is telling us that He should not come as an unexpected thief for us, His believers. He wants us to expect Him any time! When He says that He is coming unto us, I believe that He is talking both about our physical death and His second coming.

Of course, for both events, we do not know the hour. However, He wants us to be ready for it at any time! The IF THEREFORE in Revelations 3:3 follows verse two of the letter to the church in Sardis. It tells us to be watchful and strengthen the godly things in our lives: those things which remain, but are ready to die out. For God has not found our doings perfect before Him! This is also very appropriate for us today here in America. The church is degenerating in worldliness and becoming lukewarm. We are not watchful!

I am always singing the "if" verse from Romans 8:11: "If the same Spirit that raised Christ up from the dead dwells in us, it shall quicken our mortal bodies IF that Spirit dwells in you." It is my prayer that all of you will be a peculiar people and have your mortal bodies quickened by the Spirit of Christ.

THE SWORD OF GOD
AND THE EAR OF MAN

"For the Word of God is quick and powerful and sharper than any two edged sword, piercing even to the dividing asunder of the soul and spirit and of the joints and marrow and is a discerner of the thoughts and intents of the heart" (Hebrews 4:12).

The word "sword" in the Bible can mean any kind of violence or stands for the Word of God, as in this verse. Since our mission in the northern Philippines, this scripture became very meaningful to me. A great portion of northern Luzon Island was under control of the communist rebel army called NPA (New Peoples Army). Therefore, the government troops had many check points on the roads. When they stopped our 4-wheel drive truck, they always asked "Do you have any weapons?" My standard answer always was "Yes, I have a Thompson". Their reaction was always excited because the Thompson was a greatly desired American machine pistol. I would cautiously reach for my Thompson Chain Reference Bible and show them the lettering on my Bible. They would laugh nervously and then I would say, "Well, you are laughing at this, but do you know that this Bible is God's most effective weapon?" If they gave me a chance when I got out of the vehicle, I would show them this verse and preach a short admonition to them.

I wonder is that scripture talking about God's heart or our human heart, maybe both. The piercing and cutting is done to our heart for sure and the discerning that is also accomplished by us is so we can discern God's heart.

When God speaks to us, we need to hear with our ears and heart. The Hebrew word mostly used in the Bible for the verb "to hear" is "Shama" and according to the Hebrew scholars, the word "Shama" is very deep and has a broad meaning. It is not only talking about hearing with our human ears, but also with our hearts. Hearing with our hearts can be done without audible sound.

"Shama" stands for hearing with an attitude of obedience and doing what it tells us to do. Secondly, it also implies a willingness to proclaim and tell to others what we are hearting and I believe that that is what I am doing by sending you my short articles.

I often wondered why in the narrative of the suffering of Jesus, the sword and the ear are mentioned in the Gospels (Luke 22:36 and Matthew 26:51). The declaration of Jesus was kind of mysterious. It is apparent that even the disciples did not understand that Jesus was not talking about a sword made from steel when He told them to go and buy one. I believe that Jesus was talking about the spiritual sword which is the Word of God. He was actually saying, go and get a Bible! The reaction of "Lord, we have two" shows their misunderstanding and Jesus dismissed it by "It is enough".

Following the story of the arrest of Jesus, we are told that Peter drew his sword and cut off the servant's ear. To me, this also has a great symbolic meaning. It indicates that the persecutors were not able to hear God's Word but by reattaching the servant's ear, He is showing that the purpose of the suffering is to restore our spiritual hearing!

Matthew 10:24 shows again the double meaning of the sword. "I came not to send peace but a sword". When the Prophet Simon prophecies about the dedication of the child Jesus, he said "Yes, a sword shall pierce through thine soul, that the thoughts of many hearts may be revealed" thus confirming Hebrews 4:12.

The double meaning of the biblical sword is also evident in the book of Revelation. Revelation 1:16, 2:12 and 12:16, God is talking about His spiritual sword, while in Revelation 6:18 and 19:21, I believe it is an actual steel sword to kill! So, let us hear God's Word and be slain spiritually by God. In the list of the curses of God, when disobedient, we also can be slain physically by a violent sword. However, who would want that to happen? It could happen to America when we continue to be disobedient to God's word as a nation. Pray for God's mercy!

OUR BLESSED HOPE AND DOUBT

In Dutch, we have the word "hoop" for the English word "hope" and it can be used as a verb or a noun. As a verb, it means that we have a desire and expectation that something will happen in the future. But as far as I understand it, it is not a sure thing. It might or might not happen. However, I discovered that when the Bible uses the word "hope", especially in the New Testament, it usually indicates certainty?

For instance, when Titus 2:13 states, "Looking for that blessed hope and glorious appearing of the great God and our Savior, the Lord Jesus Christ", it expresses complete certainty. There are also many other scriptures indicating that the word "hope" does not include any doubts. 1 Timothy 1:1 states that Jesus Christ is our Hope.

Hebrews 6:11 is speaking about "our full assurance of hope unto the end". There does not seem to be any doubt that when God uses the concept of hope in the New Testament, it means full assurance. That is why we can sing, "Blessed assurance, Jesus is mine". In Hebrews 6:18, we are told to lay hold upon the hope set before us, because God has made an immutable promise and He never lies. Romans 8:24 tells us more what hope is: "For we are saved in this hope, but hope that is seen is not hope. For why does one still hope for what he sees? For if we hope for what we do not see, we eagerly wait for it with perseverance."

The opposite of hope seems to be despair and is caused by doubt and who wants to be in that situation? The story of Jesus and Peter walking on the water shows Peter in despair because he was sinking. Jesus rebukes him for his doubt (Matthew 14:21). It seems that the reason why our word "hope" does not indicate certainty is our human doubt and God does not like our doubt.

James calls our doubt "double-mindedness" and wavering. It states that when we are like that, we are like a wave of the sea and tossed by the wind (James 1:6). The next verse tells us that we should not think that we can receive anything from God when we are in a wavering condition. We should purify our hearts when we are double-minded (James 4:8).

Doubt seems to be a very human trait and we are sometimes hypocritical about it. The expression "doubting Thomas" is often used to label a person who is having doubts. Since we all seem to have some doubts sometimes, who are we to throw the first stone at someone? The term "doubting Thomas" is already unfair. Consider that Thomas in the Bible did not doubt any worse than the other disciples. Jesus had told them to handle Him and see His wounds when they did not believe (Luke 24:37-39). Thomas was not there at that time. To his credit, he uttered a great confession "My Lord and my God".

I am so glad that Jesus said at that time "Blessed are those who have not seen but yet believe". (John 20:29) So we as believers and followers of Jesus Christ can be assured that we are being blessed. I do believe, Hallelujah! He has risen and is my Lord and Savior and my God. I do hope and pray that He is yours also!

NEW TESTAMENT GIVING

Most evangelicals seem to agree that we are not any longer under the Law of Sin and Death, called the Mosaic Law. However, many are quick to bring out that tithing was instituted way before the Law was given and that it was already practiced by Abraham. In the light of what the New Testament teaches on giving, is this a valuable argument to keep teaching to tithe? I do not think so!

The second argument tithing teachers bring up is that Jesus and the disciples were most likely tithing and that Jesus was teaching to do so. The first part is probably correct, but to imply that Jesus is teaching us to tithe is spurious. When Jesus was rebuking the Pharisee in Matthew 23:23 and Luke 11:42, He added that they "ought" to do that because the Mosaic Law was still in force. He had not shed his blood yet to seal the New Covenant. In Luke 18:12, He rebukes the self-righteousness of the praying Pharisee for claiming to tithe. Therefore, the gospels cannot be used for defending tithing teaching.

Ever since the Reformation, evangelicals have been teaching to tithe, but it is very obvious that the blessing of the Lord does not rest upon this. Throughout history and now after almost 500 years of this teaching, the average giving of the believer is less than 2%. The Lord is closing the ears of His children and it is high time that we wake up to this fact!

The Lord is giving us very clear instructions in the New Testament:

First: He expects us to give our all, willingly, cheerfully and as a reasonable service. Realizing that everything we have belongs to him, Romans 11:36 states: "For of Him and through Him and to Him are ALL THINGS" and Romans 12:1-3 is beseeching us to give our entire selves as a living sacrifice. He expects to get interest in addition to the talents He has given us as stewards.

Second: 2 Corinthians 9:7 gives us the basic principle as to how to give. "So let EACH ONE GIVE AS HE PURPOSES IN HIS HEART", not grudgingly or of necessity for God loves a cheerful giver". Verse 6 explains that we need to give bountifully in order to have the beautiful promise of verse 8, "And God is able to make ALL grace abound toward you, that you ALWAYS having ALL sufficiency in ALL THINGS, may have an abundance for every good work". The whole of 2 Corinthians 9 are the instructions on giving, while chapter 8 tells us that He expects us to give out of what we have and not from what we do not have (not even presumptuous "faith promises").

Third: Then in 1 Corinthians 16:1-3, we are instructed to give regularly and proportionately "the first day of the week" and "as he may prosper". Now proportionality does not mean a set percentage for every one. It means in proportion to the burden it puts on you. This principle is even practiced by the not so kindhearted IRS. They have a lower rate for poor people than the richer ones. A set rate for everyone would be actually out of proportion.

Fourth: Malachi 3:10 mentions "God's storehouse". The original Hebrew word used is "owtsar", which is translated as depository or treasure. Of course, He is speaking allegorical. Malachi is the only place where this Hebrew word is used. The question arises, "What is the store house of God?" The best biblical answer is: the place from which our Father pours out His blessings upon His children. Where does He Live? In His temple! Who are His temple? The bodies of His children, the believers, who make up the Church, the Body of Christ.

To claim that our group or organization is the only or best storehouse really shows a great lack of understanding what the real church actually is. It is the worldwide Universal Church of Christ and His Body. The local church or organization should be a part of this, but sadly enough that is not always the case.

Fifth: Since everything we are and have came from God and belongs to Him and is going to Him, we have to make sure that we love Him with all our hearts, soul and mind. And as such live our lives for Him and in obedience to Him (Romans 11:6), hereby returning His talent with interest. That way we can and must look upon the needed expenditures for ourselves and our family, which He entrusted to us, as expenditures for the Lord's Kingdom. Of course, we need to guard against ungodly presumptuousness.

Most scriptures quoted here are related to practical money giving, but are also including the principle of 100% giving. Having pointed out all this, I must say that it is possible that the Lord directs your heart to give 10% in the church offering. Make sure you obey. But most likely, he will ask you for much more since He always seems to use finances as a test of our faith and obedience.

APOSTASY

There are many things which have led to the degeneration of the Protestant Church. But two issues have caused the major damage. The Greek Bible mentions the word "apostasies" from which we get the word "apostasy" which actually means falling away. Before I deal with these issues, we need to establish an important biblical fact. Our God is a God who always from the beginning of His creation wanted all of mankind to have eternal life with Him! The best biblical word I remember is the word "whosoever", from John 3:16, but of course, there are many other verses telling us that God wants everybody to be saved from hellfire (example 2 Peter 3:9).

The first issue I want to treat here is the biblical concept of predestination. The New Testament King James mentions this word four times: in Romans 8:29, 8:30 and in Ephesians 1:5 and 1:11. In all four verses, God is assuring us that He wants us to have eternal life with Him. The unfortunate idea has sprung up however, that it only pertains to believers, because Paul's letter is directed to the believers in Rome and Ephesus. But this is a wrong conclusion. Based on the light of my opening statement, some people claim that Apostle Paul was wrong in several of his writings, but the

Word of God states in 1 Corinthians 14:37, "The things I write are the commandments of the Lord!" If it was true that God wanted only believers to have eternal life with Him, He would be contradicting Himself and He never does that! Our Lord never predestinated millions of people to hellfire!

Then there is the doctrine of the so-called "free will of men". It seems that predestination clashes with this idea. I said "it seems" because it really does not, if we have the correct understanding of our so-called free will of men. I stated before, in my article "The Sovereignty of God", that the term "free will" is actually a misnomer. Because of that, the wrong idea has developed that man can decide whatever he likes without interference of God.

It is true that the Bible indicates that mankind must choose (Deuteronomy 30:19, Joshua 24:15, 1 Kings 18:21, Exodus 34:26). He also calls unbelieving sinners to repentance many times (Jeremiah 33:15, Ezekiel 33:11, Hosea 6:1). In Ezekiel, He even states that he has no pleasure in the death of the wicked! This requires a response from mankind and they have to make a choice. Jesus Himself gave divine invitations to everyone (Matthew 22:3, Luke 14:17, Revelation 3:20). We as Christians cannot even claim that we have chosen Jesus because He says in John 15:16, "You have not chosen me but I have chosen you". When I looked up the word "chosen" in God's Word, I was astounded that 99 percent of the many times it is mentioned, the Lord is doing the choosing about man and things! Therefore, our choice is our response to the Lord who is choosing us and He did it before we became Christians, "When we were yet sinners, Jesus Christ died for us" (Romans 5:8). Even if we do not respond positively, He keeps on urging us for a long time.

Out of wrong thinking about predestination also has come the idea that some people are born with a body which is bound to keep sinning. I am referring here to so-called modern science and specifically medical scientists, who are telling us that homosexuality is inborn and can be inherited. They also claim this for kleptomania (stealing), diverse addictions and sex perversion. So now, many homosexuals are claiming that they cannot help it because God made them that way!

Although it is a biblical fact that we are all born in sin and that our natural tendency is to sin against God, the Bible tells us also that we do not have to remain that way. Through belief in Jesus, we can become a new creature and then sin shall not have dominion over us (Romans 6:9-12). Praise God! He never destined us to hell!

The second issue which has caused great damage to the Protestant Church is the practice of "Clericalism". The biblical concept of the priesthood of all believers seems to have all but flown out of the window. The reformation started strongly with this concept, but today we find clericalism rampant. An old Webster dictionary gives this rebuking definition for the word, "An effort and system of ordained clergy to maintain influence and power." Today, we have mainly pastors in churches that are doing and controlling everything.

To begin with, the word "clergy" is not in the Bible! It mentions "Laos" which means laity. There are elders, deacons and bishops, but bishop is just another word for elder. There is no such thing as a head elder. Jesus is the only head in the church. But again, today the larger churches have head pastors and assistant pastors. The Bible states that God Himself has given to the church apostles, prophets, evangelists, teacher and pastors (Ephesians 4:11). We also find this five-fold leadership ministry in 1

Corinthians 12:28. Today, however, most churches ignore this five-fold leadership ministry completely. It is being said by some pastors that they never could find the four other ministers in their congregation, but are they really looking for them? The word "pastor" is found in the New Testament only one time and that in the five-fold ministry of Ephesians 4:11. Multiple ruling elders, however, are mentioned many times.

The result of this has been devastating to the Church. We are producing bench-warmers out of the Laos. Mainly, people who want to be entertained and never bring another person to Christ. They seldom or never hear the admonition to produce fruit in the form of new converts. They are like detached branches who are gathered and burned like Jesus said in John 15:6. Bearing fruit is done for the purpose of propagation and multiplication! It is very urgent for us as a Church to return to the concept of the priesthood of all believers, so that every believer can become an effective minister for Christ (1 Peter 2:9).

FAITH

God's Word tells us that "the just" shall live by faith (Romans 1:17 and Habakkuk 2:4), but we must know who are "the just". According to Romans 10:9-10, we are justified when we believe with our heart that Jesus is Lord and confess it with our mouth. Do you qualify under this condition? Then the next question is: What is faith? Also on this, the Lord gives us a clear definition, "Now faith is the substance of things hoped for, the evidence of things not seen" (Hebrews 11:1). The NIV translates it like this: "Faith is being sure of things hoped for and certain of what we do not see".

The next thing that we as believers need to know is: how do we obtain this faith? Well, our Lord tells the brethren that He has given each one the measure of faith (Romans 12:3). In addition, Romans 10:17 says, "Faith cometh by hearing and hearing the Word of God". Therefore, we should realize that we cannot work up faith by ourselves. It has to come from God.

Faith is an absolute necessity for a Christian. Hebrews 11:6 tells us that without faith it is impossible to please God. Do you want to please God? I sure hope so! We have to use our measure of faith knowing that God has given it to us. If you feel weak in your faith, you can ask the Lord to increase it. The father of the demoniac son and the Apostles asked for an increased faith and the Lord honored it.

Also, we should exercise our measure of faith so that it can grow and get stronger. It will atrophy if we do not exercise it. When the Apostles asked, "Jesus how to do the works of God", Jesus answer was "This is the work of God, that you believe in Him who He has sent" (John 6:28). It is our fundamental duty to exercise our faith daily. We cannot receive anything from the Lord without faith (James 1:6-7). Jesus told us to have faith in God. All major Bible translations say faith in God because the Greek grammar requires the Greek word pivstin to be translated as "in" when it points to a subject. Otherwise, it can be translated as "of". This is according to Greek language scholars.

However, some well known radio and TV evangelists seem to have different Bibles and teach that we should have the faith "of" God. Then they base a whole false doctrine on this mysterious force called faith, which even God had to have in order to create everything. They ignore the fact that God is all powerful and sovereign and is the giver of faith. He does not need faith Himself! But they insist that when we do have this mysterious faith "of" God, we can do much what God is doing! The result of this teaching is that our God is brought down to the human level and men's capacity is glorified. It hurts the idea that God is all powerful and completely sovereign. He is the GIVER OF FAITH and does not need it Himself! God lists "faith" in Galatians 5:22 as part of the seven fruits of the Spirit, but also as one of the nine gifts of the Spirit in

1 Corinthians 12:9.

I gather from this that as a fruit, it starts small and must grow in maturity over time. There is no thing like instant fruit! As a gift of faith, He is indicating that He makes spurts of extra faith available when needed, sometimes when He wants to use believers for a miracle. To end this meditation on faith, remember and make sure to be found in Him, not having my own righteousness, which is of the Law, but that which is through the faith of Christ, the righteous which is of God by faith (Philippians 3:9). Therefore being justified by faith, we have peace with God through our Lord Jesus Christ, that you may have this peace in abundance is my prayer.

THE BLESSINGS OF GOD

God makes many promises in His Word, especially concerning His blessings. To look up when and how He blesses a person is certainly a rewarding and fruitful project. It gives a born-again believer a stronger faith, knowing that he or she fulfils certain conditions set by God in order to receive His special blessings.

First of all, a person who comes to believe in Christ is greatly blessed with eternal life (John 3:16). Most all additional blessings are attached to this. John 20:29 tells us that we are blessed when we believe in Christ without having seen Him. In the book of Psalms alone, there are seventeen definite promises of blessings. I recommend that one looks up the blessings of God in a good concordance, like Young's Analytical. I will list here some Psalms which have to do with blessings when we are saved: Psalm 1:1; 32:1, 65:4; 84:4-5; 89:15.

Then there are many other blessed promises, speaking about trusting God, fearing God, considering the poor, making a joyful sound, etc. One I found most remarkable is Psalm 94:12, "Blessed is the man the Lord chastens!" It goes along what God tells us in Hebrew12:6. He shows His love for us when we get disciplined. Also, hearing and doing

God's Word is mentioned several times. One command which is not obeyed much any more is not polluting the Sabbath.

The New Testament is also full of God's promised blessings. Matthew 5:3-11 lists nine blessings! Some other remarkable blessings: If you hunger and weep (Luke 6:21); when other hate you (verse 12); hearing ears and seeing eyes are also mentioned. Watching and waiting for His coming will also be greatly rewarded. If you want to get more blessed, then give (Acts 20:25). One I have liked always very much is James 1:25, "looking and continuing in the perfect law of liberty". Finally, I close with Revelation 1:3, God is blessing the one who reads the words of this prophecy listen to the message and obey it.